Praise for Confes

MW01136489

"Powerful story that will i. lead their teams." *JON GORDON New York Times Bestselling author of The Energy Bus*

"Kate Leavell's important coaching memoir details her experiment with relentless positivity and the amazing results she got from it. The signature image I have of Kate as a coach is her team at halftime smiling and laughing, hanging on each other while hearing about the good things they were doing. Meanwhile the opposing team is sitting with heads down while their coach yelled at them about all the mistakes they made. And, of course Kate's team won that game. As this delightful and insightful book makes plain, Kate Leavell is the kind of coach that every youth athlete needs!" *JIM THOMPSON, Founder and CEO Positive Coaching Alliance*

"Kate's honesty, coaching wisdom and many nuggets of quotable moments makes this a must read for new and experienced coaches alike of all sports. Completely puts coaching and teaching kids into its proper perspective. I am a much better coach having read this book." *KEITH BRISOTTI, Co-Founder Route 66 Lacrosse, St Louis, MO*

"Thanks to you, I am now beginning to think I am not the only lone voice screaming in the forest. With your enlightened guidance in my hip pocket I will be ready when preparation meets opportunity." *BOB PANKE, US Lacrosse Coaches Education Trainer, Head Coach Varsity Girls Lacrosse*

"Kate's honest account of her path to discovery and purposeful culture creation will inspire leaders to tackle the culture challenges in their organizations through positive and results-driven methods." *DAVE CONORD, Vice President of Professional & Leadership Development, Long & Foster Companies*

Kate Leavell's coaching strategies promote a love for the sport of lacrosse which ultimately leads to longevity and progress in a player's game. I had the unique fortune of having Kate as an instructor at the US Lacrosse Coaching Certification Class and, later, having her as my daughter's coach. In my certification class, Kate taught us how to take common drills that enhance skills and make them fun. She did this by using lots of props, games and positive reinforcement. I loved the class and was eager to apply this to the teams I coached and supported. We started a U11 Lacrosse team and used Kate's technique and process of making lacrosse "fun". Our girls LOVED it and were eager to have practice. They surprised us all and asked if we could add a day of practice each week. I was apprehensive at first. Would these girls not be able to grasp the fundamentals and take it seriously if it was all about fun? They did, and I am confident thru our practice plans that were based around keeping it fun, the team excelled. Opponents and Parents were impressed by our first-year team. In addition, as an assistant coach for the U15 team, we had great success using these same principles and techniques. Let's face it players of any age like to have fun and when they are having fun you have their attention. I was thrilled when my daughter ended up on Kate's travel lacrosse team. Jessie was not used to props and games at a practice. Initially she was concerned would the team be ready for a tournament? She said, "this is the most fun I have ever had on a lacrosse field but I am not sure how we will do at the tournament". The girls ended up winning the Championship game at their tournament. Jessie has never shown so much improvement in such a short time working with any coach!!! I used to think if the girls wanted to be good, drills needed to be serious and very structured. I have found a greater success in my coaching and have seen an even greater success in my daughter's progress by using Kate Leavell's coaching techniques.
Kristen

Confessions of an Imperfect Coach

An Experiment in Team Culture that Changed Everything.

Kate Leavell

This book is dedicated to Michael, Drew, and Meredith. May you always have a place to play where you can love the game, love the journey, and love yourselves.

Copyright © 2017 by Kate Leavell

All rights reserved. No part of this publication may be reproduced, distributed, or transmitted in any form or by any means, including photocopying, recording, or other electronic or mechanical methods, without the prior written permission of the publisher, except in the case of brief quotations embodied in critical reviews and certain other noncommercial uses permitted by copyright law. For permission requests, write to the publisher, addressed "Attention: Permissions Coordinator," at the address below.
kate@kateleavell.com

www.kateleavell.com

Ordering Information:
Quantity sales. Special discounts are available on quantity purchases by corporations, associations, and others. For details, contact the publisher at the address above.
Orders by U.S. trade bookstores and wholesalers. Please contact kate@kateleavell.com

ISBN-13: 978-1973923923

Table of Contents

Confessions of an Imperfect Coach

Introduction

I watched my son's soccer coach, a former professional soccer player, struggle through a U7 practice. Kids weren't paying attention. The drills were boring. The instruction wasn't clear. I could see him getting flustered and I could see my son starting to get fidgety. I wanted to help him, but he didn't want any help. I had just entered my first battle of youth sports and I had no idea that I'd barely scratched the surface.

I was a nanny at one time, I had worked at kids' summer camp almost every summer, I'm a mom, I've organized plenty of organized kid activities, I played many sports. I can do better than this, I thought to myself.

So, I did what any parent does who has no idea what they're about to get into, I volunteered to coach the next season. In many ways, it wasn't much different than those summer camp activities I had organized in the past. The planning and teaching were very similar. But there was something starkly different with youth and high school team coaching that I didn't face at camp. Something I was altogether unprepared for.

Pressure. Pressure from parents, coaches, admin, other teams, records, trophies, tournaments with brackets, angry sidelines on either side, large fees and investments from families, culture destruction, and power struggles. Pressure and Microscope. As I moved my way up through different age and competitive levels of coaching youth through college, I learned every day how much harder it is than it looks. That there's more to this than I realized as a player, or a parent on the sideline. A lot more. I was influencing kids on a daily basis; often spending more one-on-one time with them than their own families or friends. What I say shapes the self-esteem of the athletes I work with, and dramatically influence their ability to love the game. But with all that pressure on me, and all those skills that need to be taught; who has time to frame a perfect interaction every single time? I felt set up to fail.

Despite my ability to lead a fun practice, filled with drills, skills, games, fun, and what I hoped was a healthy amount of motivation, I found myself struggling to find peace within my team's structure. I was always putting out fires, feeling frustrated or attacked, or just plain lost in a culture that seemed to run the team instead of the other way around.

I didn't even know that culture was the problem. What's culture? This is a sport! I wanted to teach them how to play.

"Come on kids, work hard, learn what I'm teaching, compete and get over it already! No I said get water after the...no after...no...hello!! Come back over here! No put that down, stop throwing your... Ok get on the line, you're all running! Wait...are you crying? Oh, for crying out loud..."

If you've ever coached sports you've probably enjoyed the movie, *Kicking and Screaming* with Will Ferrell more than the average person. Ever buy your team birds as a gift, wished you could hire Ditka as your assistant, or daydreamed about walking off a truck covered in aprons from a butcher's shop hoping the other team would forfeit? Probably not, but it's still fun to watch! If you have no idea what I'm talking about, you may want to go find this movie and watch it. You'll either thank me or hate me later.

I didn't find my way to writing about coaching by any accident. My life took a series of turns, and what I believe were divine interventions, and taught me a thing or two about where I was failing, repeatedly. I was lost, to the extent that I began to spend every free moment I had studying and testing culture through my leadership roles. This culture thing was beating me, and as a competitive person, I wasn't ok with that. It was taking something I loved and destroying it, turning it into something that was beating me down.

I think it's ok to fail; more than that, it's necessary. But don't just fail, grow. And don't just grow, share it, own it, and help others with it. That's why I write. Not because I'm a perfect coach, but rather just the opposite. I'm an imperfect coach;

Confessions of an Imperfect Coach

failing, learning, and finding a better way. This is my story, my journey, my lessons, and my perspective as an imperfect coach determined to do right by the people, players, families, kids, and staff that I'm leading.

I was missing an important piece in the coaching puzzle. I had fun, kindness, care, knowledge, dedication, organization, planning, wins galore, and handfuls of adjustments. Sounds pretty good, right? Those things were all there, but I didn't know how to apply them. My list was in the wrong order. My execution was inconsistent. My team had no buy in. My parents had no idea what I was doing. The miscommunications and misunderstandings were a disaster. My culture was building itself and that's not going to hold up in the long run. Negativity was seeping into our team, no matter how I tried to dress it up on the outside. A wormy apple can be beautiful on the outside and rotting inside all at the same time before the effects begin to show. We were running through winning streaks with a rotting, wormy center, and eventually; it caught up with us.

It all began with the implosion of a team that left me with a decision to make. If I do something, I want to do it well and be all in. I had to figure this out, or stop coaching. I couldn't continue this way, I knew that for sure.

That quest led me to the Positivity Experiment and that experiment changed everything. It was written in a journal as the season unfolded. My transformation was shaped with every shift in mindset, as things I had believed my whole life were suddenly upside down.

After that Experiment, I had a new way of coaching, of looking at things and seeing what is possible. I had written my story down and shared it with some people. But I still felt timid to speak out for my cause. I'd had one successful season based around positivity and I wanted to tell everyone it worked. But the real world was often less receptive to letting go of trophy seeking. I was still learning how to implement it in new situations and how to relate it to everyone. My voice was small and only reaching to those close to me. I had nothing pushing me out of my comfort zone. I let it sit, printed on a corner of my website gathering dust.

This is when divine intervention stepped in once again, when second chances at life bring clarity and focus to a mission. I set out to learn about culture, to become a better coach. What

I got in return, was a better life. Not an easier one, not one without adversity or disappointments or mistakes, but one filled with gratitude and perspective.

The Positivity
Experiment

"The Positivity Experiment"

"I still haven't fully let the enormity of this situation settle in my mind, because my heart is still so incredibly full. I know that I want to shout from the rooftops that we're doing this wrong. That the very thing we want will come if we focus on the player first. That as scary as it is to let go of outcomes, we must. That the reward for being brave enough to lead the heart instead of the scoreboard, is reaching a potential far beyond anything we could have mapped out. That we're building people, experiences, not trophy cases. I will shout this from the rooftops. You will hear my voice until my voice gives out, we can do better. We must." Kate Leavell

Implosion of a team culture

I don't know the exact day I started to lose a grip on the culture of my team. It wasn't as though an event happened and then everything went south. It was slow, like a drip in a shallow sink with a clogged drain. The little puddle was hardly noticeable at first. It seemed like such a little thing, not worthy of checking out when so many other projects needed my attention. But unattended, the drip started to become a slow, steady stream. The water in the sink was getting closer to the top. And then one day, it overflowed and there was no way to get the water back up into the sink. It was spilling over, running through my fingers, picking up momentum. It was too late, I'd let it go too long.

But I do know the season when it started to unravel. It started off the first day I was watching my team play in a preseason league. Not able to coach until the official start of the season, I was stuck on the parent sideline as a spectator, helplessly watching the disaster unfold. Weeks out from tryouts, preseason ranking had us in an unprecedented 4th place in the state. I could feel the pressure starting to build as the first whistle blew; players were out of position, slow, and out of shape. Dropped passes, missed cuts, over running ground balls, and turning over every possession.

This wasn't a team living up to the expectations of a top ranking; there was a lot of work to be done and I was anxious to get started. I knew how to get them there, I knew I could teach the skills they needed, move the puzzle pieces around. We could take that 4 ranking and blow past it, I wanted to be in that State Final, to make history.

Though I didn't yell at my players, which isn't really a part of my personality, I did keep my expectations high. Potentially impossibly high, but that push brought about an incredible learning curve. The wins were driving the team on, but they also overshadowed any potential culture issues that were growing in the shadows. Until one day, when the wins weren't enough, when the wins were no longer sweet but bitter.

It took me a few years of coaching to realize that I'm not coaching robots, but high school athletes. My efforts to eradicate their up and down emotional roller coasters and incessant boundary testing was driving us into a pit of conflict. My lack of understanding culture led me to control what I could in the only way I knew how. I needed order and perfection, no questioning, no alternate Plan B. I built a plan and it had to work; we would make it work. On the scoreboard we were creating miracles, breaking records, turning an unknown area into a powerhouse. But the joy of it was slowly being sucked out of it for everyone. I started losing their focus at practice, gave more breaks, delivered more speeches about why this was important, and scratching my head wondering where the intensity was going.

Even before I had any grasp on culture building, I'd always believed that mistakes were a sign of someone trying to improve and I had no ill feelings towards those mess ups. The problem was tied to my fixation on those mistakes. Yes, good you made a mistake, lets fix it. Let's drill this until it's perfect. After a while, all any of us saw were these mistakes that needed to be fixed. As soon as we conquered one, we moved onto the next mistake. There was no end, it was a mission with no reward at the end unless we reached perfection – an unobtainable goal.

Some of the players were falling behind, and as they started to drift back or lose interest, get frustrated, distracted or fall into a trap of negativity, they were being left behind. Left behind by the team, by me, by our momentum. It was easy to blame their lack of progress on their effort. I was giving them the corrections they needed. They weren't making them. They appeared to be uncoachable. A deep divide grew on our bench. A field of exhausted, perfection-driven chess pieces carrying out my plans, and a bench of hopeless, defeated players whose dreams seemed out of reach. The lack of attention, communication, nurturing for the players who'd lost their drive was rotting. Like a carton of old strawberries, everything the rot touched started to rot along with it. It wasn't long before I realized I was in over my head.

Confessions of an Imperfect Coach

I brought games to practice. I introduced feedback meetings. I added in policies and structure midseason – that made things worse. I planned team building activities, but the cliques that were developing kept any team building from happening. Then we'd practice, and I'd dig into the mistakes, offering little patience for those who'd fallen behind and were pulling us down. If they cared they'd work on their own. Right? If it was important they would fix it and not just complain. It didn't matter what I tried, games ended with someone crying. Crying about playing time, something they took the wrong way, even trying to point out something they did well was getting questioned. A parent or two on the sideline red faced and shouting no matter how well we had done, a microscope was put over me and I went into defensive mode. Though not an unusual trap for high school coaches to fall into, I was at a loss for what was going wrong. I loved these girls. Why weren't they seeing that? Was I supposed to stop correcting them? Stop teaching? Offer them false praise and give up on building this program all together and treat it like a club sport because they couldn't handle the pressure?

We won our conference title for the first time in history that season. It had been a rough game with not enough calls, so the girls were feeling pretty beat up. The team was breaking down, yelling at each other, walking off the field and asking for subs due to mental stress rather than physical exhaustion. At the end of the game we wanted to take a picture of the team to commemorate the big win. Only about 4 players gathered for the pictures, the others said they didn't care. I'd lost my team, I had tried every trick I had in my bag but lasting change was beyond my reach. It started sinking in that this isn't just about teaching a sport. Coaching is so much bigger than that.

We were still winning, still breaking records, still climbing. It was the one consistent positive I could grab onto, and so my focus became more lasered onto the one thing I thought was controllable. I knew how to win. I told myself that I wasn't going to let that slip by me. If I had to drag every player through the playoffs, we were going to get what I knew we were capable of reaching. I could eliminate the mistakes, we'd get there. I became even more focused on what we were doing wrong. I used to call that "coaching." Identify mistake, drill it from every angle until it works, and the strong players would show up, would get it done.

Now I call that destroying, failing, forgetting my purpose. But I didn't know any other way then.

The thing I hadn't learned about culture is that it rots more than just the bench. It destroys more than the players getting left behind. It causes more than drama, attitudes, and frustration. It also does something to your playing quality. As our team headed into a playoff game poised to send us to State, a game we'd easily won in the regular season and had every reason to believe we'd beat more easily the second time around; there was something in the air that was palpable. I knew we were going to lose. I knew it in my core. I turned around and looked at my players as we prepared to take the field and scanned their faces. They were hollow. Nothing but the frustrations, hurt, undealt with misunderstandings, rumors, and confusion hung in the air as we counted down the pregame cheer. I'd coached these girls since they were middle schoolers. They loved me then, when we had fun and celebrated learning. That's not at all what I saw in their faces now...they didn't love me anymore. It hurt to know my lack of understanding on nurturing athletes and developing relationships while striving to win had brought us here. Not because I didn't want to be that kind of leader, but because I couldn't figure out how. I saw winning on one end of the spectrum, and fun/positivity on the other end. I thought I had to choose. I was flip flopping back and forth like a rag doll – fun/positive one day, irritated and firm the next driving relentlessly forward.

They ran hard, breathless and sweaty, but their hearts were not there. We fell. I felt the true impact of a broken culture as our record came crashing down around us. I was helpless. I loved every single one of those players but I hadn't made them believe that they were valuable for who they are and not just for what they do. Every mistake they made was another step toward the defeat and end of that season.

I stood on that field for a while after that game, gently kicking up the turf pellets and watching the sun disappear. It was the moment I saw all the water on the floor from that overflowing sink. I vowed to figure this out before I ever coached another team. I stepped down as the coach at the end of the season, we were moving to another state, but even if we were staying I wasn't sure I could survive another season. My heart broke as I left that field, knowing I'd failed these kids, I vowed to never let wins, titles, records, or headlines become more important than any player.

At that point, I only knew where I was failing, but I had no idea what to do about it. It wasn't that I didn't care enough, in fact it was throwing me into a depression I fought to understand. But I needed a direction, and I didn't know where to look. I picked up some coaching books, but mostly they said to have boundaries, be tough, hold them accountable. I had no problem with that part! I probably needed less of that, but that's a lesson I still had to learn as well.

I believe in divine intervention. I believe that people are put into our lives for a reason. That's what led to the Positivity Experiment. That's what started a journey for me that has changed everything. Not just my coaching, but the way I look at life. And it wasn't just once, but twice that stand out to me. Once where I met a person with the perspective and guidance I needed, and the second time where I came face to face with myself, my limitations, my need for urgency in living out my purpose because life is short.

My journey through the past 3 years has been one of transformation. One immediate as my mindset and perspective shifted, and the other of daily lessons through doing reflections on doing it wrong, doing it right, and a lot of in between. I became a student of culture, of finding balance, of putting first things first and not allowing my emotions or my pride rule my decisions no matter how hard they fight to get out in front.

Sometimes the answer is sent directly, a gift that you can't ignore. I was seeking answers, and on a trip home from a lacrosse clinic a voice stopped me in the airport that became the catalyst for my transformation as a coach. "Hey, do you know the US Lacrosse team?" (I had on my US Lacrosse Jacket) It was best-selling author and speaker, former lacrosse player, and all around awesome person, Jon Gordon. Like my father, Jon had played lacrosse at Cornell. He was involved in Fellowship of Christian Athletes (FCA) and he wrote and spoke about culture. He and I had a lot in common, except that **he had the answers and I had the questions.** It was exactly what I needed. Jon sent me several of his books. I opened *The Energy Bus* first and then didn't stop reading until I'd finished every book. I drove over to the book store and bought the rest of his books and finished them, *The Soup, The Seed, The No Complaining Rule, The Energy Bus, and Training Camp*, inside of a week. I was like a parched person in the dessert finally getting a drink of water. It was exactly what I needed and not at all what I expected.

Like so many others, I assumed that positivity was soft, that culture building was more about being a fake cheerleader than being real. But his approach was eye opening. Face the negativity, head on. Compete, drive, build. It was anything but weak. It was inspiring. As I approached a new season with a brand-new team; I had an idea. I would run an experiment, do something I'd never have had the courage to do before. No one knew me in this state, I had just moved in, and there was nothing to lose. I didn't feel the pressure to win, I thought maybe I could change my focus and see if I couldn't figure this culture thing out one day at a time. This began the positivity experiment.

The experiment focused around a couple of key factors. First and foremost, I decided not to tell anyone I was doing it. I would show them, model it, encourage it, but not "say" it. So often we talk about culture, but that's where it ends. If I didn't tell them what I was doing, I thought that maybe if it didn't work I could save my pride. But later I realized that not telling them was a huge key to making sure I didn't just use words, that actions had to take place.

The second part was that I made a commitment that when a choice came up that conflicted between chasing a win, title, award, or recognition, I would choose to honor culture and my players as people first. No matter how hard it was. Secretly I wondered if I could actually do this, but I set out to do it anyway. Hoping I was less shallow than I felt; that I had more character somewhere in there to lose graciously, whatever that looked like.

Third, I chose to point out what we were doing well the entire season. I decided to stop looking at our mistakes, but to see where we were doing well and then teaching where we could improve. I went from constant correction to constant encouragement and celebration. I would write down positive statements on what we will do better, it changed the way I interacted and talked to my players. It changed the way they listened to me.

Confessions of an Imperfect Coach

Lastly, I decided to journal and reflect on the experiment as the season unfolded. This way I could look back, process it, see what's working and what isn't working. When I say I was determined to never let culture destroy another one of my teams, I meant it with every piece of me. Many of us love our players, our sport, our jobs and roles as coaches. I wasn't the only coach who was lost trying to translate that into effective coaching without consenting to just lose all the time with a smile. I wanted both, but for now, I was prepared to go all-in for culture and let the rest come as it may.

The following entries are real time journals from my experiment. To this day; I can still feel every emotion and mindset shift as I became a completely new kind of leader, one who has never looked back. It was a shift that cannot be undone, a transformation so strong that I spent the next 3 years writing for coaches, parents, and players on how there is a better way to love, live, and learn through sports again. I don't want anyone to stand on that field kicking up turf pellets seeing that sink overflow the way I did. It's become my mission, it's given me a voice.

March 1st
Pre-Season Play Day
First games with my new team

For a coach who is a perfectionist, this is a tough experiment to carry out. I mean, how on Earth are we going to become the powerhouse I feel driven to bring together if we can't focus on mistakes? I have expectations from parents and coaches around me to make miracles happen, after all. I am in a newer lacrosse area, I have experience in this sport, a track record of success and I'm from Maryland, that's enough to raise the expectations right there even if I didn't know a thing! If I don't focus on mistakes, we can't improve! If we don't improve, I could fail, and failure is definitely a *No Go* for me. More stress...more stress...I used everything I could to push these thoughts aside.

But the experiment began anyway this weekend, and I had to find a way to get the job done without pointing out any mistakes on or off the field. Our first game series was no ordinary start to the season. It was a 3-game tournament against teams in a higher class than us. It was freezing, our starting goalie was still in basketball season so we had a freshman, brand new to playing goalie, starting in the cage along with several other 9th graders on the starting Varsity line up. There was plenty of room for mistakes and stress this weekend, but I vowed to myself I would hold true to my promise, even if I had to shut my eyes to not see the mistakes.

Every time out, each half time talk and pregame talk, was completely focused on what we did right, what we can do in future games and on players being given the opportunity to share positive encouragements. No mistakes were mentioned, not once. I talked less, listened more, gave more high fives than I want to admit and saw faces looking back at me eager to hear every word I had to say. This certainly didn't feel anything like my last experience, but then again, we are a team still in the honeymoon period. There's no way this can last.

I wasn't sure if it was just the new team, the Southern air, or what, but my stress level was the lowest it has ever been in a game. I'm calling that a plus no matter what else happens. Even when we were down a few goals, the girls never got down on themselves, they saw solutions and opportunities to improve and they did. We beat a team we were fully expected to fall to, and then, we beat another team who had been beating everyone else. We were surprising ourselves, and apparently everyone else who wanted to know if we had recruited some new players. Two games down and I could hear parents from teams that would face us later in the season making remarks about how this year this team looked like a whole different school. I felt calm and focused, as I noticed the lists of what was happening in the game began to shift from my usual scouting for mistakes, to finding solutions, and with that, the adjustments we could make started to get much easier to see. I wasn't cluttered with frustration or piles of mistakes.

The third game we played was against a travel team that was by far a better skilled team than we were. They play year-round, and had traveled from Tennessee to play in the tournament. In the first 3 minutes, we were down 4 to 0. My stress level started to rise, I KNEW eventually all this *"ignoring mistakes"* couldn't hold up against a real challenge. But I reminded myself of my promise and I studied the field looking again for opportunity instead of mistakes. We rallied, threw a few goals back at them, and slowed down their fierce momentum. After a hard fight, even though we lost, we managed to pop 7 goals into the net in that game, more than anyone else had scored on this team. We had come together, something that my previous team had struggled with for years because under pressure; the team's culture will either create a deep sense of team unity or a gaping hole filled with defeat and negativity.

At the end of each game, we started a new tradition called Celebrations and I want to keep it going the rest of the season. We gather in a circle immediately after the handshakes and players take turns giving each other shout-outs, celebrations of everything that we saw in that game. Things like, this person had a ton of ground balls, this person really hustled, this person fell down – rolled around and still didn't drop the ball. Or this person fell down and dropped that ball, but it was really funny to watch and they had a great attitude about it, the goalie never got down on herself, etc. There was no talk of what we did wrong, because, in fact, there were no mistakes. Our perspective would allow us to see only opportunities to learn. I never told them we weren't focusing on mistakes, so I was not expecting the players to stay so positive. But they reflected exactly what I was giving them. I kept talking about positive things and focusing on solutions and they did it right back and with each other without ever being cued to do it. I wasn't expecting that at all. I thought it was harder to get teams to lose the attitudes and the blame. I've been lecturing my teams about it, and here I see all I needed to do was model it consistently.

Immediately after that loss, we got into our circle; the third and last circle of the weekend, and said our Celebrations. Despite a 7-17 score, every player left that game with a smile on her face and excitement for the learning opportunities at the next practice. No tears and no calls about playing time. I know this team struggled with culture with their last coach. I'd heard some crazy stories about the drama and what I was getting into when I came. I didn't just happen to pick up a perfect, happy, bonded team. I had some very difficult talks with some seriously negative players who have since shifted into leaders with the hopes of a team atmosphere that was fun, safe, and better than the last season's mess. This shift has been happening since we started practicing 3 weeks ago. My first day, I went home and put my head in my pillow and prayed for patience as I struggled to keep my word. It's been getting easier. Thinking about it now, after the first week I haven't gone home from a practice frustrated. That's actually amazing!

My husband, who was in the stands at each game, told me something at the end of this weekend of games that really struck me. He began to describe to me what he found to be a really interesting juxtaposition of coaching styles going on during the post-game with each team. One was our team, smiling and gathered together, celebrating each other, shouting out things we loved about our teammates performances, and looking for opportunities to meet the next challenge. The other team, with their heads down, seated with the coach standing over them, and yelling about the mistakes they made.

I hadn't thought about the difference that could be seen from the parents and spectators point of view, and it has energized me further to keep this experiment going so that I can see how we can have players benefit, but maybe also benefit the culture of this sport as a whole by touching the spectators, parents and umpires. I felt confident leaving that field that our team was going to play better in the long run and I'm holding onto the promise to myself that this season would remain positive as long as I could manage it.

March 12
The Next Game

Fast-forward...it's been a few weeks and we are onto our first official, non-tournament game of the season. We woke up to a dreary, quite cold day that was forecasting gusts of up to 40 MPH winds, temps in the 30's, and some pregame rain that softened up the grass field. Did I mention this team never plays on grass? We have several turf fields, even a turf baseball field, what's grass? Mud only complicates things at this point.

As I arrived at the field, I assessed our team. They seemed to have their mind on other things, everyone was a bit scattered and distracted, and the entire warm up felt off. Feeling confident that we would pull it together and do what we needed to do, I ignored signs of a team not ready to play and watched the game start.

Several goals hit the back of our net within the first minutes of the game, unanswered and uncontested. After our rally at the tournament, I was feeling calmer than usual about the score but as time went on the game of catch up was starting to make everyone jittery. It wasn't until half time that we got fully into our groove, got the ball in our possession, and found the net. They struggled with numb hands and, finally, what became driven spirits. We managed to get ourselves an opportunity to pull out a win, not once, or twice, but in 3 over time periods. It ended in a Sudden Death shot, score and disappointing loss for us.

There's something about Sudden Death, or Sudden Victory as it's called now, that can bring instant, overwhelming, joy and relief; or an instant crushing blow of disappointment, and there is never a buffer for it. I have always dreaded any games with overtime, they always end with too much adrenaline and a sleepless night either way it goes.

Immediately after that game, we had a team talk. I remembered my promise, but was struggling to not point out obvious mistakes. I reminded myself that these girls know the mistakes, they learned them first hand on that field, and that what they actually needed from me was direction, hope, and a little push to execute the skills they have worked so hard on. So, the post-game talk was all about our intensity level, and where we want to focus that intensity. Can we give more at practice? Can we give more during the warm up? Are we really leaving it all out there? Are we using the knowledge that's being presented at each practice to better ourselves, and can we leave each practice and each game and say, "today I became a better lacrosse player, a better teammate, and more prepared than I was yesterday?" True to the amazing character that my players have, they all thanked me as they left from that post game talk, they wanted to learn, and they craved direction. These players, they are not ordinary high school players showing up to play a new sport, these are fierce athletes. They may not always execute what they have learned, but they aren't lazy, or not paying attention, they're just learning and gaining experience and beginning to grow into what I know will be a force to be reckoned with by the time playoffs come around.

But then, I forgot to do our Celebration circle. I forgot. I FORGOT. I was crushed at the realization. When I got home, even though I felt really good about the post-game talk, I also realized that I had fallen into an old trap; the one that places emphasis on winning and forgot that these players are humans, girls with emotions and emotional tanks, girls that are self-conscious and doubt themselves, girls that internalize everything and that struggle with self-esteem. They indeed did many things right that game, including coming back from what could have been a devastating score deficit.

Those celebrations are all about lifting our players up, and no matter what the game or how many missteps we take, there is always something to celebrate...in games, in our jobs, our relationships, and in the bigger picture of life. So, at the next practice, despite having very limited time on the turf due to a shortened schedule, and the look of, "are you crazy?" from my other coach, I still insisted that we start practice with our Celebration circle that we had missed after the game.

We will lose more games at some point this season, and I hope I won't forget again to let my players leave with hopes,

Confessions of an Imperfect Coach

dreams, and a belief that they are of value even when they lose. We are a team, regardless of the outcome of our games, we must learn to live life positively in any situation, because there is always something to celebrate and keep going forward for. As soon as we stop looking forward, we find ourselves entwined with the past, trapped and struggling to move on, ask any goalie what that's like!

Our next two games were at our home field and gave us celebrations that came easily and with lots of smiles. The weather was beautiful, the refs were fantastic both nights keeping everything in order and safe, and both sides of coaches were happy with them... (wow that never happens!) The first game was a shut out requiring about 10 minutes of stalling just to keep from being unsportsmanlike with the score, and the second game ended up wrapping up quite the same as the first. It was almost, dare I say, boring? Everyone got lots of playing time, many people scored goals, had assists, had defensive turnovers, and got to show their stuff out there on the turf those nights. This is when my experiment is easy to keep up with, when everything is all wins and sunshine. In the back of my mind, I know we haven't been tested. I'm worried about that first challenge and what it will do to our happy family atmosphere. I'm worried that even if we stay united, there's no way we can win against a tougher team if I can't motivate with a more powerful stance. Will they really stay this self-motivated when things get hard? Can I handle losing when I know I could have pushed harder and gotten the win? These are the things swirling around in my head.

The next week is going to be a bit trickier, playing a team that dominates and is ranked much higher than us. A team that not only normally beats us, but that beats us by deficits greater than 10, sometimes, even close to 20 goals. This is going to be another test on the Positivity Experiment. After that triple overtime loss and then such easy games, I'm not sure we are ready for this kind of pressure.

March 19th
The Test

3 days left to prepare for Saturday's game and the talk at practice today was all about defining moments and how on any given day, any team can win or lose. We talked about basketball brackets, and how so many of them fall apart due to major upsets, and how much we want to be that major upset this weekend. In the back of my mind, I wondered if there might be a danger in getting their hopes up, would I lose their trust if we get clobbered? In the past, I have focused on reality and more down to earth goals against hard teams, but this experiment is based on faith and the pursuit of something great. I'm not sure if I'm on the right track here, but feeling in my gut that gunning for a dream is better than walking in, content with the possibility of a loss. I have continued to feed into that hope that Saturday could in fact, be our day! I felt confident that we could at least put up a good fight, if not actually pull off the Win, but these are humans and not robots, and...any team, any given day...

March 22
The Big Game Day

It's every coach's dream that when they put their faith into their players, the players live up to expectations and deliver when it counts. Going into a game as an underdog, the day after Mercer took the 3 seeded Duke out of the playoffs as a 14 seed in 2014, we were inspired to reach outside of our comfort zone and go for a lofty goal. Normally on this type of game, we would set a goal of holding the other team to a certain amount of goals and keeping the game close. But not this team, not this year. We wanted it all, we wanted the win.

During the warm up, the girls' faces were tight, serious, and I knew this wasn't the culture we were building; it would take away from the positive drive we've been focused on. Normally I might have seen those straight faces as focus, even encouraged it as an intimidation factor – hey look how serious we are about beating you today! But I've seen nerves before, and this was definitely a case of serious pregame jitters. Before the last section of the warm up, I called the girls in, I asked them if they were anxious and they confirmed that they were. I asked them to take the adrenaline and channel it into energy, and to remember why we are here. Because honestly, if you don't love this sport, what are we doing here? Players that have forgotten the fun of the chase, the thrill of little celebrations throughout the game cannot play at their full potential. If it's not fun to beat this team, then why bother? Wow, did I just say that? What's happening to me!

But the truth is, there is no big money prize or huge trophy at the end of this game. When the score board says we win; I will be a happy coach Yes, I'd love to pull it off. But I'm not really focused on that board this season. If the journey isn't fun, teach you a little something about life, create some fantastic memories, then we're wasting our time here.

So, I sent them to get some water and to come back onto the field and run through a competitive 7v7, but smiling because they want to be here. To focus on making this fun, but with an emphasis on practicing what we know and the confidence that we have prepared to the best of our ability.

And they did. Wow, I just can't explain what they did. The shift when they came back out by pure suggestion of enjoying themselves instead of accusing them of coming out flat or not wanting to play blew my mind.

Just shortly before halftime, we had scored to put us in the lead by one goal. The other team had no idea what was going on, fully expecting this to be a blowout game; they were scrambling, yelling, frustrated. 30 seconds remained on the clock, and I was pretty sure the other team was going to get a shot off if they won the draw. Something about a counting down clock that rattles a defense and inspires a fast break like nothing else. And score they did just as the clock ran out, leaving us back to a tie at the break.

With a tie score at half time, what we really needed was to rally. There weren't many adjustments we could make, because what we were doing was working. We were executing our skills, we were fighting hard, but we had to find something deeper. This other team was better, more experienced, but we were holding them off. We needed to find something we didn't know we had, and with our culture strong I wanted to do something I'd never been able to do, I wanted to find it and use it to win. Win with something more intangible than skill.

Our half time talk was a bit unusual. I knew the other team was likely getting a handful of mistakes pointed out, reasons they weren't able to pull away, reasons they were failing. I could hear the other coach yelling, I heard what he was saying, that they were a better team, that they didn't care. What do I have that the other team doesn't have? And then it hit me. I have hope, I have belief, I have a team that acts on the power of suggestion just like in our warm ups, and I knew I could hand it out freely right there on the turf to each one of my players.

Defeat comes naturally, my role is to bring out their best, not judge them for their worst. That half time was full of smiles, and celebrations with only a few changes for the second half in our

Confessions of an Imperfect Coach

attack set up. That's all they needed. Then I set them free to see what passion, belief, and dreams can do to a tie score. The problem? We lost 3 of our 4 starting defenders just before or at half time. One to a knee injury, another two a double yellow card for stepping on the crease (weird!) and the third had to leave for a band concert. There I was putting out 3 brand new defenders on a tie score in a game we were supposed to be wrecked in. We didn't even mention it at half time, it was as though we had no challenges, we focused on putting our best out there and nothing else.

Second half started and we scored in 30 seconds right off the draw. And then again, and again, until 4 unanswered goals hit the back of the net. In that 25 minutes, the other team only managed to scrape in 2 more goals to our 6. I saw teamwork and hustle on that field that I don't see very often at the high school level. Under a huge amount of pressure, total exhaustion, and being pushed to their limits, I never saw these girls back down, get negative, hang their head or utter one negative statement on that field. I couldn't soak it all in, I'd never seen that before. What was happening?

Yes, I have been telling them to be positive, focus on what we can do, and expand the areas that we have room for improvement. I told them to believe that we can do it, that heart mixed with preparation and action can make you do things that seem out of reach. I told them there are no limits, only those we set for ourselves, that we can be so much more than we know.

I told them all those things that I've been told before but didn't know if I believed really worked. A little part of me that still doubted that this experiment could give me a happy team AND wins, is in complete and utter awe. I want wins, oh boy, do I want wins. But after that toxic season in my past, I want happy players even more. Though I'd never tell the other coaches or players this, I'm willing to sacrifice wins if necessary to have these girls leave the season saying it was the best memories they have from high school and that they learned a little something about how to conquer life's challenges and ups and downs by being on this team. I'm no longer willing to compromise a positive atmosphere for the sake of games, points or titles. Never again.

It's mid-season and I'm realizing that we just might get both. We just might do something rather incredible here. Maybe this experiment is more than an experiment, maybe its life changing, maybe its inspiring teenage girls to have faith, confidence and go for dreams, and maybe, just maybe, its doing something amazing to me as well. I can feel something going on that I can't explain just yet, but it feels like perspective and a little like joy - and it's not just happening during lacrosse, its touching a whole lot more.

******

(I wrote this post while on a plane, and I sat in my little plane seat typing this with tears streaming down my face. This was the beginning of a huge shift. The shift didn't happen right after the game, it happened when I was writing about it, reflecting and realizing the depth of what was happening. I still remember exactly how it felt to realize how much deeper coaching impacts players and their leaders).

May 1
14 and 2

With limited time and access to the JV team, the experiment has pulled the Varsity team in a starkly different direction than our training team that wasn't experiencing our positive foundation. As the Varsity players became closer, more unified and more determined, the JV team began to rip apart at the seams with inner conflict, lack of attendance, lack of energy or drive and pockets of developing drama.

The importance of beginning the season with the expectations of positivity and focusing only on opportunities has become very clear, as putting out fires that were growing exponentially started taking its toll on the JV coaches. Our varsity captains began to mentor the younger girls in an attempt to redirect them, and though it helped; it just wasn't enough to chase out the negativity that had filled the void there. I took mental notes to remember that we cannot lapse in our dedication to driving the team from the beginning in the right direction as a program. Those girls who come up next year will not be in the same place as the rest of the team because of that misstep in my experiment.

But for Varsity, the culture had been growing and thriving over the 4 months we had together. Game after game, the team rallied, each one holding a special value because it was something these girls had never done. Our pregame speech became a mantra, do something we've never done, show the world what 20 girls on a mission, fully focused and devoted can really do when you put us together on a field. The usual panic that happens when a team is down at the beginning of a game just wasn't there. I didn't feel it, but I noticed that I didn't feel it. It was remarkable. As the other teams would start yelling and screaming at each other, this team was busy coming up with solutions, almost immune to the pressure. I had adjustments for the team, but as the close of the season approached, these empowered girls rarely needed them. They had already figured out how to adjust on their own on the field, meet together after goals, and turn the games around. They were telling me how they would fix it, I was just giving them a thumbs-up, like, go ahead, you got this!

Second half teams are so often the sign of a healthy team culture. I've had both kinds, and the biggest difference between them was the team unity and how it either rots or flourishes under pressure. With our strong base, our second halves were the most fun and beautifully played part of almost all our games, no matter how flat or slow we may have come out at the start. The usual teenage issues were still there. The crazy schedules. The school day, boys, and friendship drama wasn't any less, but on the field they rallied past those distractions rather than folding from them.

At the close of the regular season now it's occurring to me that we have not lost a game since the one where we forgot to do our Celebration circle. That was a million years ago. It never occurred to me that would be our last loss of the season, that we wouldn't lose again after that triple overtime in the freezing rain. I would never have believed it if you told me this team that finished in the bottom of the pile last year would be on a 12-game winning streak while not focusing on winning, but rather a fantastic playing experience.

We are about to roll into the playoffs, 4 games would take us to win State, where just one loss means this incredible experiment and season will be over and we have to say goodbye to our seniors.

Even with my incredible faith in this team, I'm not quite expecting to get that far. This team has never even been to the Final Four, usually knocked out in the first game of playoffs. But *what if* has entered my mind. I've learned better than to doubt the power of culture. What if we could win the state tournament on faith and with team unity, that's crazy right? Some of the teams we have to face are much faster than us, have players with more experience, have won the state championship year after year, and we haven't faced anyone that would give us that sort of challenge yet to gauge what we are capable of.

Confessions of an Imperfect Coach

So the irony in all this, is that the very first game we face in playoffs is against the very team that gave us our last loss 13 games ago in overtime. We now must go back and look that loss in the eyes and see if we've grown over the last two months.

As we enter an uncertain future during playoffs, the hardest part of the experiment is nearing and one I hadn't really thought to prepare for. What do I say before a game that could end the season at the last whistle? Only one team in the state ends their season with a win, how do I guide this team to leave a possible loss still feeling like they succeeded? How do I help them try their best to win and dream without setting them up for disappointment? I have less than a week to figure this out. The close of this season is going to be bittersweet for me, these girls have changed everything about the way I coach this sport and how I feel about my job. And I know this is a year I will never ever forget. At the end of the last game, that last loss, there are often tears of disappointment in the players' eyes. Even the toughest of them will break down from the let-down after firing out everything they have on that field only to fall short. This year at the final whistle, I really believe that any tears will be shed over the end of what we all want to go on forever with each other on this team and not because of disappointment over a loss. Maybe this is the focus, maybe this is what will carry us through – the desire to keep us together for one more day before we have to say goodbye, and not on the actual win.

May 10th
The Playoffs

I'm sitting here at my desk filled with all kinds of crazy emotions, so many that I am still unsure which one is the most prevalent. One more day, that was our theme for the first playoff game. We didn't focus on the scoreboard, we focused on extending what has already been an amazing season. When the final horn blew at the end of the game, the very team that had given us our only regular season loss, had just been defeated by our amazing team with a score of 20 to 6. This was a rite of passage for us, it meant we had grown over the last few months that we were prepared and united to get this victory, and we can only hope, the next one as well.

But now, I sit here just hours before playoff game number two, the game that would put us into the Final Four and I'm feeling more emotional than usual. It occurs to me that this is the exact position I was in at the final game with my last team. We were poised to win and get into the Final Four, but the team was not united. I was empty after a season of being picked apart by parents and a new athletic director and a team that I had been coaching since 5 years before as young girls. I went into that game feeling like I had nothing to give and the players faces reflected the same. What should have been an easy win became a defeat, and it was the last time that I stepped onto that field that had felt like a second home to me. It was my last season as a head coach before moving, it was the last time I wanted to set foot onto another turf field, ever. It's the only time in my life I wanted to quit and walk away in the middle of a game and just run as far as I could until I collapsed. It was despair, I had nothing left.

I know that this team is different, our unity is beyond anything I have every experienced, we ARE prepared, but that awful sinking reminder of this phase with my last team is pulling at my emotions today. I have several times pulled out a picture

Confessions of an Imperfect Coach

of my team to remind myself that this is a new day, a new team and a chance to finish what I started in a positive and encouraging atmosphere. I am not the same person, and my leadership style is completely different.

It was supposed to be gorgeous and sunny today, but all day the wind and the storm clouds have been hanging and whipping around, which feels fitting for the war going on inside my head. I know that once I step in front of this team, once I see their faces, their joy and their love of this game; the past will be washed away, that win or lose I know they will put everything they have out there, that they can do no less. What will our focus be tonight, *one more day* I suppose still fits, none of us want this to be over just yet.

As the pregame rituals began, the warm up, the line up calls, the pregame prayers said, the leaves were flying through the sky all around us as dark storm clouds rolled in pinching out the light of early evening. The storm sirens went off and the team ran to take cover in the shed near the field. As though the pregame jitters weren't high enough, this delay heightened the anxiety swelling inside both coaches and players. This is worst-case-scenario for our team. We are mainly a passing team, and when it rains, our edge to move the ball is taken away. I knew the first 10 minutes would be bad, maybe even very bad, but I sat in that shed praying for the rain to pass over us quickly. As we waited, the girls circled up and played games, my goal was to keep them distracted and having fun and to keep myself sane...if possible!

Only 5 or so minutes passed while we sat in that shed when the all clear bell rang and we took that field, in pouring, soaking rain, wind, and dark skies. We couldn't seem to stay on our feet, or connect our passes; the other team was all over us. At half-time the score sat at 3 to 7, and we headed back to the shed to prepare for the second half.

The strangest calm came over me during the first half. Despite goal after goal being scored on our team in the first half, something in my gut just said to be calm, that this team never fails to come together when faced with a challenge. So, the half time talk was about challenges and fear. We were playing with caution, fear of dropping the ball, missing a shot, fear of making mistakes. The second half was to be about going for it, leaving those fears aside, and putting ourselves out there. Then we talked about challenges...the first challenge was getting through a team that beat us in the regular season, and now this challenge was to rise when our ability to move the ball was struggling with soaking wet pockets in our sticks and slippery cleats. This was the time to put aside the first half, and prove that we deserve to be here, to get one more day together and show what we are capable of. We will never know if we are capable of winning the State Championship game if we don't get there, and we want to know if we've got the stuff to get it done.

Team culture is the recipe for disaster or success under pressure. For the first time in a long time, team culture was our saving grace, it was the catalyst in our turn around that made even the lingering soccer fans in the stadium who know nothing of lacrosse, stand up and start screaming in excitement for us.

That second half we came back from a 4-point deficit to take the lead in a matter of minutes after the first whistle, and we never looked back. The final score was 13-10 after we outscored them 10-3 in those closing 25 minutes. As the girls stormed the field with that win, I was filled with an overwhelming sense of being a part of something so much bigger than just a lacrosse game. What we just did was not a normal response to being that defeated at half time, it was a rally of the heart and soul of teammates who don't know the meaning of giving up, who don't know mistakes, who see opportunity even when the odds are miserably out of balance in the other team's favor. I've seen these teams in movies, read about them in books. But I've never experienced it first hand, and those movies and books don't hold a candle to expressing the energy that comes from this sort of determination, unity, and devotion.

Final Four, I don't know what the future holds for us but I know that whatever it is, failure isn't even listed as one of the options. This team will win, if not on the scoreboard then in life, in love of this game, in joy from this season, in memories, friendships, connections, and confidence. They may realize it now, or many years from now, that though they've not yet played the biggest game of the season, they have already won the greatest prize.

May 14th
The last whistle means one thing, time to get ice cream!

The promise was for a team trip out for ice cream immediately following the State playoff game, no matter what the outcome. So, in a game of uncertainty, one thing was a guarantee, yumminess was coming for all of us!

-Most wins in a season
- farthest into the State playoffs than ever before even breaking into the state Final Four
-beating every rival this school ever had, beating every team that had previously dominated us by more than 10 goals consistently for years
- longest consecutive winning streak with only one in season loss that happened in over time
- most assisted goals ever in the history of the team
- most goals ever
 -less than half of the average allowed goals ever scored against this team...

On paper, this team was a miracle.

Though we hung tough for the entire first half of the State game against the 5-time state championship team, we fell in the second half unable to keep up the back and forth battle. At the end of the game, I looked at these players and they were still celebrating their amazing season. The last Celebration circle was bittersweet as we looked at our 7 seniors that would no longer be on this ride with us. The Athletic Director came down and joined the circle, giving shout outs to our players, the coaching staff, the managers, and ultimately this amazing lacrosse program. The pride on his face brought so much joy to our players and to our staff reminded me just how much bigger sports are than wins and losses. Records and streaks get attention, but teams that pull together change lives and that is why I love my job. The Athletic Director and Principal of a school coming to games might be normal in other sports, but in a school where many of the students didn't even realize there was a girls' lacrosse program...this was anything but typical. To have the Athletic Director jumping up and down in the press box with excitement is a clear sign that the positive energy that was flowing from the lax players was reaching the rest of the school, even in a sport that they still don't really understand.

I still haven't fully let the enormity of this situation settle in my mind, because my heart is still so incredibly full. I know that I want to shout from the rooftops that we're doing this wrong! As coaches, we're focused on outcomes and getting more out of our players instead of being focused on processes and giving more. That the very thing we want will come if we focus on the players first. That as scary as it is to let go of outcomes, we must. That the reward for being brave enough to lead the heart instead of the scoreboard, is reaching a potential far beyond anything we could have mapped out. That we're building people, experiences, not trophy cases. I will shout this from the rooftops. You will hear my voice until my voice gives out, we can do better. We must.

Divine Intervention
Steps in Again

Confessions of an Imperfect Coach

The Future

There are some lessons that define us, separate seasons into our lives and become a before and after. The experiment was one of those. This was another.

It is in our discomfort that we grow the most. What makes us move? We move because we need something, we are uncomfortable, we shift our position to seek something better. Comfort feels good but it's not the gift that adversity is. Everything good in my life came from some sort of struggle. I likely didn't appreciate the other things because I took them for granted and they didn't help me to grow.

I'd learned a great deal from this experiment. But I needed something or someone to tell me that time is of the essence. I needed to be uncomfortable. I felt I had figured it out, but I had barely scratched the surface. God made sure that I heard loud and clear that I couldn't be silent when I have the opportunity to share something that will benefit so many. That I couldn't wait on my message. That I had so much more to learn, I could not sit back and get comfortable.

Only a few short months after the end of the season I was diagnosed with a Pulmonary Embolism. A healthy, young adult, this wasn't anything I'd seen coming. A PE is a blood clot that travels to your lungs. In 25% of the population, the first symptom of a PE is sudden death. There's a reported 1 in 4 chance of dying from a new clot in the following 2 years if you survive the initial one, or so my doctor said.

I was sent home after a week stay at the hospital with blood thinners. But after only a few short hours back home I was losing the ability to speak or move. I couldn't control my arms or legs. I was taken by ambulance past my kids who were huddled on the steps watching me be wheeled out to the front yard with the techs calling in a stroke patient on the way. Gratefully, I was having an allergic reaction to the blood thinner and not actually having a stroke, but the fear we all went through was incredible and there I was back in the hospital for a few weeks once again.

I spent a lot of time in and out of the hospital that year. Either with my blood clotting or too thin and bleeding. I signed waivers for the meds they were giving me, putting the same ingredients in me that is in rat poison in order to keep me safe. Twice weekly appointments to make certain my medication was in check, which it almost never was.

We all know somewhere inside that life is short, that tomorrow is promised to no one, that we need to use the time we have. But like so many others, I was taking time and opportunity for granted. Here I was being told that there could be more clots, that my risk was increased, and that there's a 1 in 4 chance that my first symptom will be sudden death. Every morning I got up and literally said thank you. Every night I went to bed, praying to make it to the next day. My world was wrapped in fear, trauma, and constant ER visits from not being able to stabilize my meds. The positivity experiment was being buried under a mound of uncontrollable, outcome-based fears. The anxiety was paralyzing.

At that time, I wondered if I would be able to step back onto the field, knowing that a rogue lacrosse ball throw to the head could mean a brain hemorrhage, or torn muscle could be a bleed out. Every time my calf cramped up I had to go to the ER for a doppler scan to make sure it wasn't a DVT, and for someone who was active and usually had a sore calf just from being at the gym I began to fear working out. Fear became my one word, I hadn't chosen it, it had chosen me and I was shrinking behind it.

As I spent some time off the field, I spent some time observing, paying attention, studying and sitting at my computer, writing. This was the birth of my blog and where I found out that my message was reaching people. It started with about 5 hits on my website. I was pretty excited. But then it started to grow. 100, 500, 1000 people a day, reading sharing and emailing me their own experiences. I realized, there were lost coaches, just like me that wanted to do better or just understand why their good intentions weren't translating into their culture. Parents and players out there who were thriving off my messages the way I was from Gordon's books before I ran my experiment. I began to replace my fear with passion to grow what I had started.

I shifted my mindset. I received several emails detailing how coaches had used the information in my articles to turn around their team. I was shocked. My articles??

There's a moment where our purpose is revealed to us, and I didn't know exactly what it would look like, but I knew that what I had learned in the positivity experiment needed to apply here in life, if I was going to move forward.

You see, I needed to stop seeing roadblocks and start seeing that this adversity was just to push me outside of my comfort zone. Adversity was just there to drive me to action, and I would not waste it. The fear had become my cloak, to hide behind and the only way past it was to face it, head on.

I found courage and my voice, and not only did I begin to reach more people, but I also found my way back out on to the lacrosse field to coach. Very few know the extent of the fear I faced just go walk back onto that turf. For the next 3 years, as I lived out my dedication to continuing coaching the heart and letting go of outcomes, I wrote about my experiences, my kids experiences with their own coaches, my observations, and messages that as a coaches' education trainer I heard over and over needed to be delivered. I learned. I studied. I messed up. I confessed to my teams, I told them all the time – let's do that over, I said that wrong. Let's try this again, but better! My teams began to join in the mission to help me become a better coach, always learning. They became comfortable letting me know we needed a do over and I learned to appreciate that feedback and thrive on it instead of fearing it or trying to overpower it.

For three years I wrote articles, chapters if you will, based around lessons I've learned, inspirations, ideas, and lessons. I chose the articles that received the most feedback from readers that they had seen a new perspective, related, been touched, or shared, framed, and loved.

There is a team out there, a coach, a player, or perhaps a parent who's watching that sink spill over. Pass this along, it just might change everything for them, too.

The articles that follow are my writings as I continued to learn, seek a better way, and face my own faults as a growing, but imperfect coach.

Confessions of an Imperfect Coach

Adversity in Coaching

Encouragement for Coaches,
we all need these so I put them FIRST!

Confessions of an Imperfect Coach

Dear Coach, Please Stand.

You either stand for something, or you can slink out of the hot, uncomfortable spotlight. There's either a microscope on you, or you blend into the background, making no mark on anything around you. So often I want to wish away all the politics, the drama, the trying to please everyone, the holding players accountable while attempting the impossible task of not rocking the boat in an entitled world.

Have you ever lead a team and felt the sting of doubt creep in when some person has distorted and warped your very message into something you can't even try to recognize and pronounce it as fact? When people who haven't taken the time to know you at all, stand on the mountain top proclaiming your intentions to be unworthy?

How often do we question ourselves, our purpose, our abilities? How easy is it for us to look longingly at the hidden shadow where the safety of not standing up for something beckons us? Where we can safely encourage others to have a voice, while we stifle our own to guard our hearts. How long can we stand against the tide when we feel tired and unsure if we even matter. Are we even reaching anyone anymore? Is there still a point to all of this?

What if we were to escape the difficult culture, that all too many coaches are living in these days, for perhaps just a bit of respite from the heat. How long would we truly be happy knowing that we were turning our backs on the very kids who need our support, guidance, belief in them, cheering and leadership, only to gain a bit of comfort? And would we regretfully long for the smell of the grass, the morning chill, the whistle sounds in the background, the giggles, the high fives and the game, oh that game. Would we miss the game that we love?

There is no power, no ego to claim, no entitlement in leading or coaching; there is only service. There is no great monetary benefit, accolades, parades, statues, grand titles, or privileges to be gained when we choose to lead young athletes through learning to master a game and navigate the challenges of life.

Oh, but there is a reward. There is a bounty so large and so great that no matter how many times we may face those questioning our purpose, our motives, our passion; we must not walk away or become defeated. The reward is why we stay, why we come back, why when in the darkest most powerful windstorms we continue to stand.

This reward is unlike other awards meant for just one person, usually yourself. This reward is a waterfall that cascades from the coach to the player, to the family of the player, to the players who one day play for that player as they grow up and become a coach themselves. This reward comes back up to the coach, it reaches countless lives, it grows, it breathes, it lives in every single person that thrives in the experience they have gained. This reward doesn't sit on a shelf and gather dust. It doesn't wear out in time; it holds no limit or title. It's the fulfillment of your purpose, it has no price tag, no expiration date, no required retirement age. It's bigger than any doubter, political twister, position seeker, or power monger.

So, Stand Up, Coach. Let those who have false motives simply wash away with the tides of time. Keep reaching, stretching, growing, empowering, guiding, loving, serving, and know that challenges are but a validation that you have chosen to stand for something, for someone, for many someones.

So, Stand. Stand for every player whose life has been blessed by your service. Stand for every moment a player has blessed you in return.

So, though you may sometimes be looking longingly into the shadow, where relief and quiet lay, hear the whisper on the wind – "Dear Coach, Please Stand."

10 Reasons Volunteering to Coach Will Improve your Life

1. Kids see things for what they are, we as adults often see things for what they can or might be. While this can be motivating and useful, it can also be incredibly stressful since we often see the possible failures more often than possible victories. Kids teach us to live in the moment, to take our eyes off the outcome and to look right in front of us.

2. Teaching young players how to adapt to pressure reinforces the skills we have learned or maybe haven't learned, about keeping what's most important as our number 1 priority in every situation. Nothing keeps you more accountable to your behavior than a bench full of little eyeballs watching and emulating your every move, and stands full of parents studying you (with smart phone videos posted every other minute).

3. Kids can make anything and everything into something funny. Learning to laugh through challenges keeps us sane, lowers blood pressure and gives us perspective. No matter what mood I arrive to practice in, I always leave re-energized and generally with another inside team joke.

4. Kids have a leaky, under-developed filter. They may sometimes guard what they say, but for the most part, they are going to tell it like it is. Was that drill horrible? Did you stick your foot in your mouth and call someone by your dog's name again? Did you demo something wrong or randomly dance to a song when you thought no one was looking? Is your fly down? They noticed, and they're gonna call you out. Even your best friends may never be so honest.

5. Coaching makes us appreciate taking things down to the simplest layers. Problem solving is all we do. When we coach, we know we must break it down into manageable chunks in order to conquer large tasks, and that carries over when we leave the field as well.

6. Filling the bucket of others actually fills our own. The realization that we hold the key to a person's self-esteem

in the very words we choose is a powerful concept. Ever give a kid a genuine compliment and see their entire posture change? There's no vitamin that can feed our health like building up the confidence of a child.

7. Kids keep us young. I didn't say cool, I said young. (they will quickly point out that we aren't cool, especially if your own kid is on the team and frankly, even if they aren't our own kid...) They introduce you to Snapchat and you will find yourself in your office doing a selfie that turns your face into a tomato or switching faces with your dog. It will happen, and you will love it.

8. Coaching is about bringing people together, and that includes ourselves. It's about becoming a piece of something that has value. That builds, improves, makes memories, and ultimately steals a portion of your heart and your mind every day. That will change you. Somehow it finds a hole that needed filling and it fills it. If you haven't coached, you won't understand it and if you have, then you're likely nodding your head right now.

9. It's like playing a live chess game – building skills, arranging puzzles pieces, finding match ups. Coaching is a game for adults, except the chess pieces sometimes show up late, get distracted, need 6 bathroom trips, take your only pair of gloves, need 4 shoe lace tying breaks, and forget their equipment. SO... it's more fun, right?

10. Coaches gain more than they give when they give it all. The more a coach loves, serves and gives to their team, the more exponential is the growth on personal return. Basically – not only do you get back what you put into it, but you get more. Youth athletes haven't been tainted yet by recruiting, stats, power, money and ego; they just love the game and their friends, and their coaches. Who couldn't use a little more of that in their life??

Coaching youth sports is less about the sport and more about the development of people. If you've turned down opportunities to coach a team because you don't know the sport and feel unqualified, look at it in a different light. You're leading kids with no life experience down a road that will teach them how to navigate their future in an environment filled with fun and competition. You can learn the skills and the breakdowns of your sport in the myriad of educational sources out there – **what you really need to coach – is heart!**

It may be stressful, take up a lot of your time, and you may feel overwhelmed, but at the end of the season – you'll never be the same, you will be a better, more enlightened, and more passionate human being. Because once you have been called coach it won't last for just a season. Once you are called coach – you are one for life.

When Coaching Sucks...

Cue Julie Andrews... "I simply remember my favorite things and then I don't feel soooo badddddd"....

The smell of the grass, the perfect lines on the turf, the bright green against the woods in the background, the walk-down song, the pre-game dinners, the half-time speeches, the post-game handshakes, the matching jackets, the shared anticipation, the shared victories and defeats, the bus ride home, the comebacks, the unexpected heroes... these are a few of my favorite things!

I've been on teams throughout my life, but as I become an adult, the opportunity to be a part of a team had slowly drifted away. I found myself again and filled a hole that was missing something when I became a coach. And though I didn't know why at the time, over the years I have discovered that I thrive in a team atmosphere. I am right where I belong in the middle of a group of people all reaching to be their best, individually and together. I was growing as a person when I was part of a team. But coaching, especially in this current climate is hard. It's very hard. Sometimes coaching just, well there's no other way to say it... it just sucks.

Why do you coach? What's in it for you? What keeps you from walking away when it gets ugly? Unless you're coaching college football, I doubt you're in it for the pay or the fame or a chance at coaching professionally. Often as coaches, we look at what we are doing for our players to help them grow, learn, and develop, and as a motivator, we should. But we can become empty during a difficult season when we don't see the flip side of the equation. Yes, we are getting incredible affirming returns from seeing our players thrive, seeing them succeed, watching them overcome adversities and finding their potential. YES-those rewards are fulfilling and prove that we are coaching with purpose. But there's something else we are missing, something important that coaching does for us as a part of the team. Something we probably don't appreciate at face value unless we change our thinking.

Look at the other side. The stuff we don't like so much – those interactions with difficult parents, the new team policy that blew up on us, the witty comment that ended up hurting someone's feelings, the play that backfired, the player we let down, the player that didn't reach their potential, the team that never jelled, the playoff that never was but should have been, the misunderstanding we couldn't clear up, the power-hungry family that tried to take us out...

Those are the stretchers, the growers, the "I DON'T LIKE THIS!" moments that sharpen us and make us better if we can manage to not quit through them. We get something out of coaching that has nothing to do with the game. We become better people, better leaders, better servants. We aren't just transforming our players out there, we must let this position and this team transform **US** as well.

If I've been the same coach for 10 or 20 years, then I'm missing the incredible gift that coaching offers me to be better.

If you are staring up a wall in your coaching experience right now remember, once you can scale this wall, you'll know how to scale the next one. This struggle is going to make you more effective, stronger, and more understanding. And your team, your family, and your life will benefit every year from the growth that you allowed yourself to experience. It isn't enough to focus on the parts of coaching that you love, because even those may not keep you around through some of the darker storms coaching can bring.

You must truly be grateful for what the storm is doing for you so that you can get through it and get something beneficial out of it.

There are seasons that I've wanted to walk away because it got too hard. There are preseasons where I wondered if I'd even make it to season start day. But as Tom Hanks character in A League of their Own, so eloquently stated, **"It's supposed to be hard. If it wasn't hard everyone would do it. The hard is what makes it great."**

When you think of your WHY this season, when you picture those players transforming, your love of the game, and all that you can do for them as you serve – don't forget that you're changing too, that your transformation is a part of the process and that you're still reaching for your own potential too!

Put it in Your Story

Our lives are a series of ups and downs. Sometimes more down than up and sometimes more up than down. If perception truly is reality – if the story we are telling ourselves about the world around us and the events we experience are what is real, then we have the power to change everything, at any time, by making a choice.

One very powerful choice.

A few months ago, I was given some advice by women's advocate, ice hockey coach extraordinaire, and co-founder of the UWLX women's professional lacrosse league, Digit Murphy, that was meant to help me overcome a political coaching disappointment I was going through. She said, "Put it in your story."

As a writer, I immediately thought, *well I'm not writing a story about this, seems like a bitter and kind of miserable story to tell.* I'm only telling you because I want some sympathy and I needed to whine a little bit about it....

But she went on saying something like this; *Put it in the story about your life, when you tell who you are and how you came to be where you are.*

Digit was looking at a much bigger picture.

She was looking at what we do with the uncontrollable. Not the chapter or page we are stuck in now, but where that story goes and how we use it. Digit uses her story to create change, empower women through her voice and influence through sports, and inspire others to use their own voice.

When I see struggle, I can respond knowing it's a part of the adventure, its taking me somewhere to learn something, like all my adventures have, or I can just see it as a setback.

What's the difference maker? What is the powerful choice that we have that changes our perception and therefore our reality?

Gratitude. Everything I have faced has been a part of my ever-building story, and what makes up who I am and who I will be. How I choose to perceive challenges and adversity paints the

Confessions of an Imperfect Coach

pages in my future, and helps to clarify the pages in my past. It also reminds me that pages turn, that we do move forward, that whatever is going on, good or bad, is temporary. I choose how my story ends. I choose if I stand back up or if I quit. I choose if I see opportunities or if I see walls. I choose if I will use my stories to help others.

Whatever challenges you are facing today, *put it in your story*. Decide where it goes, what you will learn, how you can tell it in a way that helps others. You may not have control over the events around you, but you get to tell yourself what happens next.

Something Losers Say

Losing is beautiful, it's a gift, it's a learning opportunity. This reminds me of a clip from the movie Liar Liar with Jim Carey when his son makes a wish that for one day he can't lie. His son says to his dad, "my teacher says that beauty is on the inside." To which Carey's character who must now say what he really thinks responds, "That's just something ugly people say."

So, is all this talk about losing just something losers say? Because tonight we got routed 2-18; a score I haven't seen in a while, if ever, and it didn't feel like a gift if I'm being honest. There were lessons there, there were moments of triumph, everyone played, and our team culture was positive. So that part was OK. There were little celebrations that we tried to have as they unfolded. But I'm not glowing in grateful splendor now. Instead I'm here, on my blog, feeling that feeling that coaches get when we wonder if we suck at our jobs.

Every game has a loser, so why is it so hard to process it when it happens? It's the reason so many coaches ditch positivity and resort to screaming, demanding, demeaning, embarrassing, and doing anything possible to avoid it. It's miserable and it makes us question ourselves and our ability to do what we've been hired to do. It's like trying to start your car when the engine is dead and you're late for work. It's frustrating being on the losing side and feeling powerless to turn it around.

But as I sit here processing what to work on next, writing out how this losing thing is wreaking havoc on my psyche, I'm starting to see the gift I was missing while I was too busy feeling like I was failing my team. A reminder. Positivity is NOT SOFT. We don't need to trade wins for it, it's not *either or*. Positivity must go hand in hand with competition in order to be successful. There's a recipe for successful culture and programs; and like baking, a missing ingredient can turn something sweet into something bitter and hard to swallow. We can't pick and choose our philosophy based on the situation, our mood, our record, or our amounts of pressure.

We need them all.

Confessions of an Imperfect Coach

- Positive perspective on the past, present, and future (the story we tell ourselves)
- Belief in players, team, and self and the ability to do things not yet done
- Faith in the process
- Expectations and Standards
- Accountability in the controllable areas (effort, kindness, focus, being prepared)
- Communication
- Openness to new ideas, trying new things, avoiding labels

Sometimes we get focused on that positive outlook and start to go into happy land and let our expectations and standards start to slide in lieu of keeping the peace. Other times we get hung up on the standards and accountability and forget to have faith in the process, believe in ourselves, or remain positive. Like it or not, losing is a built-in part of the process for all but a historic elite few. Our philosophy, faith, and recipe for success must be constant in the face of wins and losses because both are coming our way.

Winning doesn't make us winners and losing doesn't make us losers. But losing our way, our purpose, our reason for leading these teen athletes in an attempt to control an outcome – that is what we should be losing sleep over. Not a scoreboard. Not a title, banner, or trophy; those will come and go.

And so, my fellow coaches, rest well in your purpose, strive to win but truly let go of the outcomes and let the process define your win instead.

Uncontrollable outcomes and circumstances are the number one reason for coach burnout and turnover.

I promise not to let them be mine, don't let them be yours. Winning is fleeting and only lasts until the next game where you must start the battle over. Losing stings, but is erased with that next win. My point is, neither will bring you lasting peace or destruction, so don't give them that power.

Tomorrow we return to the field to get 1% better once again.

For All the Coaches Out There
#OACAAC
(Once A Coach, Always A Coach)

If coaching success is measured by how many times we mess up and start over again, then I'm an expert. I used to think, before I started coaching, that getting out on a field and throwing out a few drills was all that coaching entailed. Like punching a time clock: show up – do the skills – go home and focus on something else. It was quite an awakening to realize coaching is more than something you do. It becomes a part of you, it grows, it brings incredible amounts of joy and sometimes frustration and sorrow. It is influenced by our own struggles and successes and we hope that it drives and builds the lives and dreams of those we have the honor to serve.

Just when I think I have it all figured out, the season is over, kids move on and I must start all over again with a new team and new personalities and skills. When the playoffs are done, it becomes plain to see that coaching doesn't end. It just renews itself and changes with our teams and with the perspective we gain from our kids who show up to practice, and from our own lives and experiences.

I never anticipated the difficulty of saying goodbye to kids that have impacted my life in so many ways at the end of a season, or after four or more years of them being a big part of my daily thoughts, prayers and struggles together. How hard it is to recreate something amazing every season with new and changing personalities?

Through all the ups and downs in a coach's life we learn, we mess up, we frustrate (and become frustrated by) a few parents and players and mostly ourselves, and we find out exactly what we are made of. No matter how hard it can get, coaches are in it for life.

You can decide to walk away, retire, take a break, but you'll never stop being a coach

Confessions of an Imperfect Coach

Parent, Player, and Coach Relationships

(building ones that last!)

Confessions of an Imperfect Coach

Meet in the Middle; Salvaging our Youth Sports Experience

There are bad coaches out there, there are misguided awful parents, there are disrespectful lazy and/or entitled players-but that's never going to change and they have been around for decades. There's a long discussion that could happen, and is happening, on the fact that it's getting worse and what's causing it. But the bulk of our problem, the one spiraling out of control, lies in the break-down occurring in the coordination of our common goals into a well-executed and communicated plan, between everyone involved in our youth programs.

Remember when coaches, parents, and players were all on the same page years ago? Me neither! And it's only getting worse as we fail to get everyone working together despite the commonality of our goals and desires.

We can't fix crazy and we can't remove egos-those aren't going anywhere. What is within our control is uniting the well-intentioned, but poorly executed system that's currently out there. By labeling all the issues in youth sports as bad people/coaches/players we make the situation a lost cause when it's actually within our reach to make marked improvements. We can salvage our youth sports, we can work around the bad eggs – I have to believe that's true.

I've heard **coaches** who I know love what they do and are out there for the love of the kids, who still belittle and demean players attempting to motivate using tough love without knowing at all that their coaching method is hurting their team. I've seen loving, caring, enthusiastic, helpful **parents** lose it when they don't understand what is going on or what the expectations are; and becoming a coach's worst nightmare. And I've seen **players** who started out loving the sport become lazy, bored, or defiant when they are constantly confused by a broken communication system and a lack of positive leadership.

All three parties-going after the same goal; all three missing the mark completely. Consistently failing one another over long periods of time crumbling our youth sports infrastructure, driving stereotypes, and making a lose-lose-lose situation for everyone.

Parents, players, and coaches are starting off already defensive as the season starts, unsure of motives, unsure of procedure, unsure of roles, while we microscope each other into misery. We can all nod at each other and say we are in this for the kids; but what does that look like? Does it look the same to all of us? Do we really believe the other is genuinely in it for the kids or are we skeptical from Day 1?

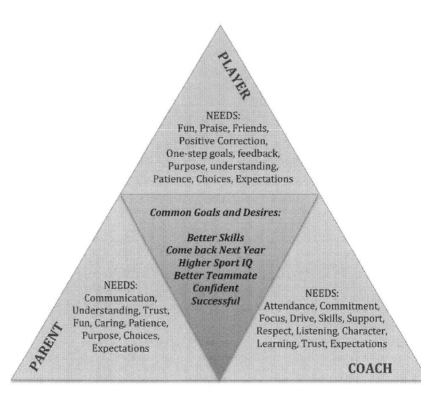

This triangle is your sports program, with the three participating components and a common center goal. When parents, players, and coaches express their needs, such as the common ones listed in the info graphic above, then a structure can be built that benefits everyone. And when everyone knows what the common goals are, there's a focus and a destination for the end of the season, as well as a measuring stick to see if you were successful in what really matters the most. Often, we get caught up in winning streaks, Facebook brags, and college scholarships as being most important when a quick look at the common goals would remind us otherwise.

Confessions of an Imperfect Coach

Many programs have a triangle where the corners are separated by a large space and no vision of common goals or the needs of each other. By meeting with all three groups and defining each segment of the triangle before the season starts, the gaps close and the unit can function more efficiently. After needs and goals are understood, then the action plan can be built and put into place – the how part of the journey. Programs that offer this structure can appeal to parents seeking a more unified and direct approach to what they are looking for and coaches can make sure they are attracting parents that are supportive of their vision.

Define the goals, put roles and communication methods in place, define the path to the goal, and meet in the middle at the desired destination.

Let's rebuild how we approach our team and program structure. PLAY ON!

Building a Wolf Pack with Parents, Players, & Coaches

We talk about lanes, roles, and boundaries between coaches, players, and parents. We each lead in our own way. Whatever it is you have to offer, there's a place to lead when we're looking at a team.

But where we lead is important if we want to build the best wolf pack, the best support system, a unified and driven group of people who know how to move forward towards goals effectively. Have a vision? You're going to need teamwork that goes beyond your roster if you want to reach it, and that's a fact.

I've been in every role, and I've experimented with leadership from different places. I've seen where leadership can become an obstacle instead of a catalyst. Something incredible happens when everyone figures out how to coordinate to make the most impact and contribute to a team's success. If someone is out of place, it can become a stampede to the end of the season while everyone trips and shouts over each other. There's often players and parents and even coaches who get left behind, sometimes before the season is even over.

WHERE TO LEAD:

COACHES: Imagine you are teaching someone to drive. You can't be in the driver's seat and teach effectively, because the student needs to do it. I can't imagine you'd want to be out in front of that car walking backwards and directing, that's certainly not where I wanted to be when my kids were driving! You can push from behind, maybe if they're stuck, but generally, you want to be in the passenger seat. You're along for the ride, giving advice, looking around for possible dangers, and encouraging them as they do well. Coaches lead without getting in the way when they are leading alongside the players, looking out for roadblocks, can see what might be chasing behind, can give direction but can also let them "do" while being out of the way so they can move forward freely or slow down as they need to. With coaches on either side of the team they can build the trail or the map. Their position keeps the team in the center and moving the right way.

CAPTAINS: Captains are a part of the team, but in a leadership role. They are leaders who also actively participate in the same roles as the rest of the team and need to be among their teammates. Captains lead from the front, by example, by doing and showing the team how to follow. Captains also mix in with the team, encourage them to move at their pace and keep up. In this role, they can also see if anyone is falling behind and feel the mood, attitudes, and feedback of the team. Captains are in touch with the team's culture and can direct that info out to the sides where the coaches are forming lanes and instructions for moving forward.

PARENTS: Parents are the reason the team doesn't stop moving. They lead from behind, cheering, praising, and pressing forward. Stepping up to help fill holes and assisting with responsibilities that hold up a team's structure. Any player who is feeling discouraged, lost, who maybe has not received the support they needed while falling to the back of the pack will be encouraged forward by a solid line of parents who are there to tell them they CAN in fact DO IT! When parents form a net, unified in supporting the entire team (not just their own child or their child's friends), then no one can fall through the cracks. When the parents commit to cheering for all of the players, the coaches, the captains, and continually having faith in their abilities to overcome, then this team simply cannot fail. Without the parents there, leading from behind, the team can scatter, lose players, lose coaches, and the captains sag to the middle and must carry the load of the team. Teams can't function without parents' support.

PLAYERS: Players are there in the center, driving forward and listening for instruction, following their captains, communicating in all directions, and connecting with those around them in order to keep pace. Players are behind the captains for a reason, because it's not only the players that need support from behind. Our captains also need the team to rally and tell them they believe in their leadership, they believe in where they are going and they are coming too!

Build a pack this year and form an indestructible culture of support. Have your team come up with an incredible vision and then come together and live it!

Leave No Room For Doubt

You want to build a program with a mission. This is your pre- try out or pre- placement speech. Leave no room for doubt. Make no apologies.

Instead of rules and regulations to keep people in line, build the expectation before they set foot on the field. Let them decide to get off the bus before your journey even begins. Build something that inspires your program's vision.

Be direct, firm, inspiring and unwavering. Be resolute in your mission, fluid in your process, and driven by a greater purpose than the game.

"Before anyone takes this field today, before any parents write a single check or commit to a schedule of driving back and forth, buying snacks and proudly wearing your team gear... there's something you need to know.

You aren't trying out for a sport today. You aren't even just trying out for a team. You are trying out for a program and our program has a mission.

To make this team you have to be a right fit athletically, emotionally, and you need to believe in where we are going. Athletic ability and talent will help you be successful in plays but does not determine your success as a teammate.

So I'm going to tell you what that mission is and as we decide if your athlete, and your family is right for us, it's important that you decide if this is the mission and program that you want to be a part of. We are going to the end of this season together, and that's a commitment we do not take lightly.

You're not trying out for a sport. This sport is all over, opportunities at every corner to just play. It's what comes with the sport, where you want to go with it, what you hope to get from it that makes or breaks where you decide to sign up and try out to play.

We are so resolute and passionate in where we are going, that we want families who will live this mission with us. On the field, on the side line, in their public lives, in social media, in their interactions with opponents and officials.

Here is our mission:

We are building:
We believe in:
We believe the role of sports is to:
At the end of your child's experience we want them to have gained:
We believe the following are the most important traits in an athlete in our program:
We believe the role of parents, coaches, players are:

If you believe, as we do, that this is a place your child can thrive, a place you can represent as a fan, parent, and part of our mission, then we look forward to seeing your athlete out in the field today for evaluations. If not, we have a list of other programs out there in our area you can look into and find the right fit. "

Don't be caught up in those checks walking out the door. Let those not committed to your mission find the right fit for them somewhere else. In the long-run your program will thrive as those without a clear mission dissolve under pressure, drama and internal fires.

Let Parents Back Inside the Circle of Trust

Some bad egg parents have made coaches draw a hard line, cutting parents out of our communication. As a coach I understand it, and I've felt that need to escape the microscope. The majority of coaches are in the mindset that the less contact we have with parents, the less we get drug into the middle of politics that swirl around those bleachers, kitchen tables, and practice parking lots.

"Don't talk to coaches about playing time."

"Don't question where we play your kid!"

"We only want to hear from the player."

In a struggle for structure and to keep the peace, those statements have become a universal preseason expectation list set in any number of sports and at every age level. The problem is, we aren't stopping the drama. On the contrary, we are driving and feeding it, but also choosing to stay out of and ignore it.

The sentiment behind those statements is meant to be positive for the team experience. We want to let the coach do the coaching and make the tough decisions. We need to keep everyone in their lanes. We ask parents to help kids navigate life lessons, we hope to teach kids to self-advocate. Those are qualities of a strong program.

But I believe cutting the parents out is causing **more harm, not less.**

Much of the drama that starts among parents comes from misunderstandings, misreading, and misinterpretation. Without open communication, speculation runs wild and suddenly your great plan that makes total sense, but is a complete mystery to your parents becomes rumors about your ego, your intentions, and your favorites. Your closed door is simply a blindfold, it's not a solution.

It may sound like a scary idea, but try an **open-door policy** one season and see if it doesn't squash a lot of the drama. You can't stop the bully parents no matter what you do, but you can head off the well-intentioned but totally confused ones, and build a strong support system in the process. If your players' parents know that they can make an appointment with you and ask you questions about their own child, they are less likely to jump to conclusions and stir the pot with other parents. In fact, they may come to your defense because they will be armed with the truth. They are less likely to have that kitchen table talk that makes your player lose respect for your authority. They feel secure in your best interest for their child. They may still disagree with you or your coaching staff's choices, but knowledge is far less painful than ignorance when our kid's happiness is at stake.

How can we ask parents to work with their kids on life lessons, which is where we are asking them to focus, when they are confused and frustrated themselves about what's going on?

For example: "Son, I know you are frustrated about not playing much lately. The coach says you are struggling on ground balls. While I know you and I feel you are very good at grabbing them and you didn't agree when he told you that when you met with him after practice, I spoke with him for more clarification. He is noticing that you don't have great body position when you are in a group of players and attempting to scoop. That's something we can work on and maybe watch some videos together so you see what he's talking about. See if he has some suggestions for you as well at the next practice, and ask specifically what he wants you to work on." In this instance, there seems to be a miscommunication about what the coach meant when he told the player his ground balls weren't up to par. Kids are learning to interpret feedback and I can't tell you how many times the message a player is given is completely different when they get home and talk to mom and dad. Because the parent had an open door, used it, and got clarification, he could use that to work with his son on skill improvements and learning to ask more questions. Drama averted, life lesson activated, team and coach trust is stronger.

Rather than a "don't talk to the coach about playing time" speech in the preseason, try an alternative player-centric approach that **allows parents to work inside their lane** through the power of knowledge.

Example Open-Door Policy Wording:

Our coaches have an open-door policy. That means that we would like players to request a meeting with us if they have any questions. We may also request a meeting with a player if they are struggling or not playing much. We have a mutual interest in your kids becoming great athletes and want our subs as strong as our starters. Parents may also make a meeting as long as it is more than 24 hours after a game for a cooling off period. It is very possible that as a parent, you won't agree with our reasoning, but we respect you and your choice to allow and pay for your child to play for us. We believe you deserve to not feel left in the dark. We will never discuss players other than your own child or compare skills as that would be disrespectful to the team. We will not entertain any conversations that involve disrespecting the coaching staff or the knowledge and hard work of that staff. Honest, open communication is always welcome in the right setting, and so we will always respond to requests for meetings whenever a parent feels upset, confused, or needs clarification or even feedback on their child's progress.

In addition, players who are not receiving regular playing time will be asked to meet briefly with a coach once a week to go over what skills, attitude, or other adjustments are needed to earn more time. They will be given an action plan that may include work needed outside of practice. At the next meeting, the coach and player will evaluate if improvements are being seen and make corrections or additions to the plan if necessary. It may be a quick fix, or it may take a season or two. Improvement speed depends on the player's desire to work hard, the time they desire to put in, and their athletic abilities. Parents may attend these meetings but it is not necessary as they will be quick and the player will be given a written action plan to take home. Any clarifications on action plans can be talked about via a phone call with the coach if needed.

I've had hard conversations with parents. It's hard to be told by the coach that their awesome kid has been screwing around at practice, or not trying their best, or is consistently failing to improve on a specific skill. But being able to hear from the coach how much they value your child and want their child to succeed is often something parents just need to hear when their kids are struggling. No matter how hard that conversation has been, I've always come out the other side of it with a deeper bond with that family and positive unified goal to make that kid a better player. It's not just the parent that learns from these conversations. As a coach, I learn more about how my coaching style meshes with players or if they are misunderstanding something or worse, think I don't like them. My open door has saved my relationship with many players and built an unbreakable trust with them, and I'll never go back to the other way.

We need to break the **Coach vs Parent** cycle. We need to open the communication doors between our lanes. Focus instead on the need for mutual respect in these conversations, having it at appropriate times, and zero in on the common goal of keeping players motivated, growing, learning, and loving their sport. We are all in this together, and a few rotten apples aside, we really **do** want the same things.

Parents and Parent Coaches

Confessions of an Imperfect Coach

A Letter to my Former Self as a New Sports Parent

One day you're going to get in the car with your kid's water bottle that he left at home for the last time, the smell of shoulder pads and cleats coming from the back seat, and the little chunks of dirt that have been knocked loose from muddy cleats all over the once new floor mats. You're going to climb the stadium stairs one last time, listen to his name announced, watch him take the field and shoot a glance up your way and a little wave. You're going to hear the last whistle, watch the last half time talk, the last hand shake, eat your last stadium hot dog, shade out that last bright sun beam blocking your view, and then you are going to get in the car and you won't ever be back again.

Today may be the first time he sits in your lap as you lace up his cleats and then walks onto that field, and he may be terrible, he may be fantastic, he will likely have moments of both, but when it's all over he's still that piece of you that you love no matter what.

All I care about now at the end of this journey, is that he had fun, that he has memories that he cherishes rather than ones he hopes to forget. His playing time, lack of college offers that he never cared about or wanted anyway, coach philosophies, club teams, stats – none of it mattered. Not one bit. Don't waste time keeping up with the Jones's of sports parents, just love every. single. second.

When he is small, sports will seem like such a milestone and you will be in a hurry to get him into as much as you can. If he shows promise you may start looking ahead, thinking you are depriving him if you don't get him the training he deserves. Be ready, because the second it starts the comparison and expectations are instantly out of reach. Don't miss the fun, don't miss the laughs, don't miss the chance to reassure when the tears come, hug him tight, hand him an ice pack when he gets hurt and then send him back out there. And when he wants a break, when he says he misses his friends, respect that request.

Don't worry about what the coaches are doing, how the team is playing, who should be playing, if they are learning as fast as other teams, if they are a super star, or even if they are winning. Just look at them – are they happy? Are they growing, learning, reaching, and stepping outside of their comfort zone?

Because at the end of their sports experience, that's all that matters. You won't care about anything else when it's over.

There are so many things outside of sports that he loves to do, that he is so amazing at. There are so many opportunities that are going to get missed if he is training all the time. He doesn't want to play in college, that was my destiny, not his. But the things he learned playing sports he will use every day when he leaves for college next year.

Don't let him forget that he has other talents, to explore as much as possible, to focus on the things he loves but to also constantly try something different just for the experience. Don't let his self-worth become directly tied to his athletic abilities. Don't let your relationship become coach and player instead of parent and child.

Soak in every moment of every game, absorb the cheers, the goof ups, the missteps, the sometimes less than perfect effort, the sometimes mind-blowing plays, the team events, the mud, the smell, the tears, the joy, because one day it's going to be over.

You're going to miss the smell that you think you hate on that drive home from practice, you're going to miss the constant shuttling to and from practice, volunteer responsibilities and team events, you're going to miss all the time you spent worrying about team stuff instead of just relaxing and watching him love the game. You're going to remember those band-aid moments, emergency room visits, got cut from the team and then, years later, the being made captain moments. Hold on tight, and remember why he is playing, never miss an opportunity to experience the complete and total joy you get from just getting to watch him play, because it doesn't last, and it doesn't come back.

An Open Letter to my Teen Athlete

On the first day of tryouts.

Dear Son,

I know you've been anxiously awaiting today to come, the first day of your season. I've watched your excitement build. I've driven you to practices, workouts, and countless stores for gear. I've nervously watched you drive off with your newly licensed friends to preseason events. I bought you team apparel complete with logos that you proudly wear every chance you get. I wrote the checks for you to play. I've seen you work hard, I've seen you slack off because there were other things grabbing your attention. I've seen your strengths; I also know where you struggle.

I see the anxiety of the day behind your eyes and your nervous smile. I know you're worried about how you will perform, how the other players will like you, how your coach will like you. I know you're worried if you'll be in good enough shape to handle what's expected. I know you're worried about messing up in front of people, of making mistakes, of letting people down. I know that you love this game, that you play because it's something you enjoy, the challenge, the team atmosphere, the friendships, the competition. I know that more than anything you want to feel like you have succeeded, that you can master new things, that you can make us proud.

Here's what you need to know. I'm already proud of you. I already think you're one of the best. There will be days that you feel like you did nothing right, and when you come home you will find someone who just loves to watch you do your thing, to watch you play. Your teammates and your coach may be hard on you, you may struggle, you may make the wrong choices sometimes, you may fall – repeatedly.

You have my support, you have my unending desire to help you figure out how to navigate the sea of ups and downs that come with playing sports. You have my promise that I will listen, that I will love you through whatever comes, but that I won't allow you to justify poor decisions with excuses or blame. Your worth does not lie inside of what you do, how you perform, if you win, if you make a certain team, how much playing time you get, or what awards or stats come your way. Those things are for your own goals and ambitions, but are not what makes up a mother's love. There is no failure on the field that can take that away.

I expect you to work hard, to respect your teammates, coaches, opponents, and officials. To stick up for the ones that cannot stick up for themselves, to help those who struggle and need help, and to hold true to your beliefs no matter what pressures come your way. My hope is that your value will come from living out who you are on the inside, and not from the opinions of your teammates or coaches. That your decisions will be based on character and values and not on emotions or outside influences, and I will be there to help you learn how to do that along the way. Your coaches, teammates, officials, opponents, teachers, classmates, will all have opinions about you. None of those opinions define you, none of those opinions should change who you are.

My hope for you is that at the end of your high school playing career, you've built memories, friendships, a love of competition, the tools to overcome and learn from mistakes and defeat, and the drive to reach for something that is outside of your comfort zone. I hope that you bring your incredible, unique personality into the team, to help build the foundation that great teams are made of, and that you never feel like you must change who you are to make others happy.

I hope that at the end of it all, you are glad you played, you remember the friendships and not the scores, and that you move on to the next chapter with anticipation, firm in your other interests, and just a touch of sadness at saying goodbye.

Love,
Mom

Nooooo! Breaking Kids with our Sideline Jeering

I remember the exact moment I found out sports weren't about fun; the first time I ever felt humiliated doing something that I thought I loved. I was in 10th grade and tried out for the soccer team. I'd been to a soccer camp one time, but didn't really understand the strategy involved in the game. Despite being athletic and an accomplished lacrosse player, I was still learning the basics of soccer. I was really enjoying practices, competing for the ball, running hard, and pushing myself. Sometimes I felt lost in the concepts but the coach spent most of the time teaching ball handling or scrimmaging without much correction, and I didn't realize how much more there was to the game.

I remember playing Severn High School in Maryland. We were losing, it was a tough game. But I was quickly discovering that my sprinting speed combined with having fresh legs from not playing much were giving me an edge in the game. I saw an opportunity and I ran to the ball, tackled it from a player and saw nothing but open field in front of me. I heard a huge blast of cheering from my team's bench, the coach, the parents. I was suddenly very aware that I was on stage, something I'd never felt before. I was a defender, sometimes a sweeper. My job up until that point had been to use what God gave me – powerful legs! I was ordinarily told to kick that ball as hard and far as I could, and I was good at it. But I was playing midfield in this game, and I was out in front with the ball. At the sound of the cheering, I felt what can hardly be described. It was adrenaline, pride, excitement. Here I was, a bench player and I'd done something heroic. I looked ahead, readied my powerful quad muscles, fired 'em up, and kicked that ball as far ahead as I could. It soared at least 50 yards. A beautiful kick.

The cheering stopped. I immediately heard a loud shrill 'NOOOOOOO!' I can still hear it, it was 22 years ago and I can still remember exactly what it sounded like. It was followed by 'WHAT ARE YOU DOING?!?' and as the opposing goalkeeper scooped up the loose ball, I heard my name being screamed from the sideline. I hustled off, knowing I'd done something bad, feeling utterly humiliated in front of a crowd of people just seconds after feeling a surge of confidence I'd never felt before. My coach didn't tell me what I did wrong. She turned her back to me. I didn't see the field the rest of the game. No one ever explained what I clearly know now should have been a controlled fast break.

The rest of the season, instead of excitement when the ball came near me, I felt fear. It held me back, it got in my head. I was afraid of being publicly humiliated on the field in front of a crowd of people and in front of my teammates. I was more frustrated at practice, I didn't look forward to it anymore. I lost the connection with my coach. She never did tell me what I did wrong, she never apologized for humiliating me, she never took me aside and gave me some encouragement. I saw exactly what I meant to her, and it felt like nothing. I laid awake that night, haunted by it, tossing and turning, feeling so embarrassed. She probably never thought about it again.

These players are deeply affected by some of our communication choices, they are still learning how to process correction. How we do it matters. How we clean up after our mistaken outburst matters.

As a coach, this is a scenario that I try not to forget, that I try to never let myself be on the other side of. To this day, when I coach with my husband in basketball, if he yells out 'NO' onto the court after a mistake, he gets a quick slap in the leg to stop it. It's something I can't tolerate. Can you imagine yelling 'NOOOOOOO!' in front of an auditorium as your child sings a wrong note in a solo? We'd never do that because we know that would be humiliating! Yet in sports? I've never heard so many corrections, insults, frustrated NOOOOOs or groans coming from both sidelines. It may not be a coach, it might be a parent, that verbal correction given while an athlete dares to do something brave could be the stifling end to the freedom they must truly try, learn, and love what they are doing.

Corrections are best done one on one, by the coach, in a teaching environment. Are you coaching your kid? Dinner or the car ride isn't a great place to add more coaching, end the coaching with practice and go back to parent mode. Not the coach? Wait til they ask for help. Offer to play in the back yard together. Avoid giving unwanted direction, be their cheerleader instead.

Confessions of an Imperfect Coach

Think about how you communicate with your players. Next time you're at work in front of your boss imagine being called out with a verbal 'NOOOOOOOO' or yelled correction in front of the entire room and realize it's no easier for these kids. Imagine the parents screaming every time you make a correction, or a substitution, you probably wouldn't last the season under that sort of verbal thrashing. These kids need our support not our verbal frustration.

The second half of that year I transferred schools, and despite not being a great soccer player, a very awesome coach, (who had every right to cut me from a perennial state championship team), told me he was putting me on varsity because I had heart. Because he valued what I brought to the team other than my not so great understanding of the game. Because I had worked my tail off during tryouts and I had earned it. I've given that opportunity to many athletes as a return on that kindness since then. Thanks Coach Seivert!

Sick of Multi-Sport Talk. This Means More

Forget talking about multi-sport. I'm tired of that topic. Its turned into a mantra and an excuse to now require kids to play multiple sports all at the same time, all year round. Specialization on steroids. Leave it to us parents and coaches to ruin what was supposed to be a positive movement to alternate sports to protect our kids from injury and burn out. If you hated the multi-sport movement, then you'll really hate this one. It doesn't follow the current sports overdrive trend at all. In fact, it down right drops it on its head.

Instead of talking about multi-sport, let's dig deeper and commit to not ruin this one, because it's incredibly important! **How about multi-dimensional kids.** We've put sports on the ultimate pedestal. I don't know any parents whose kids aren't playing sports anymore. Either we are developing some incredible genes in this country or there are some pretty miserable, not-so-sports minded kids being dragged through year-round misery, desperately hoping no one offers them a sports scholarship so they can end the madness.

In our sports focused culture, we call our players student-athletes. But how many coaches are really hoping to share their kids with those pesky ACT, AP TESTs, other activities, Prom, jobs, family events, trips, college visits, or huge projects that are stealing their focus? Our goal is to build great teams, we understandably want their complete attention and attendance. How many times as coaches do we get frustrated because these kids have other things on their minds or taking their time? Believe me, I've felt it. I'd love to have a team full of kids who do nothing but train. I could rock that state championship every year if that's what I had. But that's called professional sports, and that's not the job we signed up for. We signed up for coaching kids, either young or through high school age and they do not owe all their free time to practicing their craft.

Have you met their teacher? They also want their students to be focused on their classes, studying outside of class, working with their partners on their projects and growing.

Maybe you've met their parents, hoping that their kids whose schedules are overwhelmingly full will spend some time with their family, get their chores done and help around the house, be responsible, come along on summer vacations and to grandma's house over the holidays, take care of their pursuits of excellence in school, sports, health, and their future.

How about their church? If that's a part of their life, then they've got a group relying on them to show up, study, share, and grow in their faith.

Maybe they happen to enjoy other activities, ones that they are having a hard time fitting in without an incredible amount of guilt because they aren't *grinding* at their sport.

Perhaps that pesky manager at their work, the one from their job that allows them to pay for the gas and the car that gets them to school and practice, hopefully some college money and valuable work experience, would like them to show up, work hard and be available and reliable for their shifts.

Our kids are living in a shifting, full, colorful world and as sports become more and more important to all of us, we are building for our growing children a world of monotone, single focus, and dare I say, obsession? I've watched a kid show up for his Eagle Scout ceremony in tears because he had been so miserably guilt tripped by his coach about missing practice before a big game. His huge accomplishment was ruined because his coach couldn't get a grip on sharing importance in our kids' lives instead of owning it.

I remember playing sports casually in the off season to stay in shape. I remember hard practices, Saturday practices, and games on the weekends. I played at top programs and we worked hard. But my schedule never came close to the demands being laid out today on our athletes. I worked at my part time job at Ledo's Pizza throughout lacrosse season. It was less hours, but I managed it and it wasn't that big of a deal. I didn't travel all summer to tournaments, but remember attending one camp, and sometimes playing a weekly league game that no one cared about and was more for fun than anything else.

I played one sport at a time in an organized program, and if you saw me playing multiple sports on the same day it was because I was at the park with my friends making up weird games and not feeling like sports were a job I needed time off from. I enjoyed playing sports in my off time, it was often my go to activity with my friends because no one was calling it *training*. There weren't any coaches and there weren't any parents, unless they were having fun playing too. I asked for advice and it was rarely offered if I wasn't seeking it. There wasn't any pressure other than my own desire to get better, and yes folks, that was enough.

I saw a family out in the park playing soccer together and at first, I had a nostalgic feeling of care-free fun in the park. It lasted about two minutes until I saw the dad start digging into that little 6 or 7-year-old about her kick being all wrong and it went downhill from there. It wasn't a fun day at the park at all, it was sport obsessed athletic training, before she could even probably write her own name.

What. Are. We. Doing?

I'm looking at young kids who probably have a ton of engineering, artistic, math and other strengths and interests, being shoved into sports that they clearly don't enjoy. Many kids we see being pushed the hardest aren't particularly athletic and may never realize what other options are out there because these days sports are THE thing. If they aren't great at it then, we just train them harder. I've never seen so many kids with their own personal training, sports specific one-on-one training, several travel teams, and 5-7 days a week of training all before even getting through middle school.

One parent said they have tried everything, but their kids isn't getting better and surely there must be another trainer somewhere I could suggest. Maybe they aren't cut out for sports?? That's OK! What happened to multi-dimension? To kids trying many new things, finding their interests, spreading their time around, learning what they like? What happened to it being OK to play sports just for fun and not for college? What happened to sports being an activity and not a job? Only a handful of kids are ELITE athletes, but we're training 'em all like that's what they have to be.

Playing sports in college is fun, don't get me wrong. But would I trade my childhood for it? **Nope.** Multi-dimensional focus is going to help our kids find out where their strengths are. If they are a super star athlete we'll know, they don't need specialized training to find that out.

So, here's the bottom line: We, as coaches, need to push our kids to be their best. But that awards ceremony for an accomplishment they spent all year or longer working towards that they must miss practice for, that huge project that is 60% of their grade that's stealing their out of practice *grind at the wall ball* time, that ACT test, or job they need to get out on time from practice for, those matter too.

Let's find a way to put sports back into the puzzle instead of throwing out all the other pieces and taking over. Multi-dimensional kids will make for a much brighter world. Only a small portion of these kids will go on to play sports even past high school. Those other activities that are cramping our style and stealing our players attention, will likely be the very skills they will use as an adult. We all need a little perspective check and multi-dimension back in our lives.

Confessions of an Imperfect Coach

Culture Building

(From the top down)

Confessions of an Imperfect Coach

Strengthen your Weak Leg. Culture FIRST

One of my most frequently asked questions is how to organize "what to teach a team" and "when" in order to find the most successful season. As I have transformed as a coach, I have changed my approach drastically and not everyone is thrilled with this answer at first, until they try it and realize it works! I used to teach Defense, then Offense, then Transition. As the season went on, I attempted to address culture issues when they arose, tell people to be positive, rely on the ones that were positive and excited to (sort of) cancel out the ones that weren't, and keep building on the skills at an incredible rate. They learned full defensive and offensive setups from Day 1 and we drilled it until it was perfection with the first game as the looming deadline. It may have been stressful...

This was quite effective in certain aspects of building a team. It brought wins early on and created very solid regular season records. The problem I was running into is that I couldn't maintain that growth curve. I was leaving some players behind who couldn't keep up. I was putting a huge amount of stress on the team to master things and ignoring the signs that come with a focus on X's and O's. Some would call it peaking too early. It was a plateau or a downhill slope right about playoff time because they were no longer hungry, no longer absorbing new info, losing interest, losing excitement, sometimes feeling unimportant, misunderstood, lost, or just plain BURNT OUT.

It's several weeks and games into our season right now and I literally just introduced our defensive strategy to my team for the first time yesterday. We spent 10 minutes or less on it just to see what it looks like. It's a defense that will take weeks to master, something they've never seen before. The offense has only been taught basic rules of engagement, a simple foundation that the team will in fact, design themselves now that they have a working knowledge of how to cycle and shift through movement. The only way to get better at that is through trial and error at game times. We are building a base. We are building it piece by piece and with enough time to make sure it sticks. Transition and stick work have been an important focus because those carry a lot of weight and need the longest to develop, master, and need daily reinforcement. But again, they aren't my primary focus as the season gets rolling.

So, what is my primary focus? Shooting? Clearing? Checking? What's the magic ingredient that gets a team to grow as much as possible in just one season? How do we make sure teams are not limping along at the end after a huge early momentum burst?

My primary focus, my main objective when a season starts is culture. **Culture comes first.** Culture creates unity, internal motivation, excitement, and a mindset that is ready to absorb and apply new knowledge effectively. Culture is what takes a team from wherever they are and propels them into wherever they can imagine and believe they can be. I changed my learning curve from a steep uphill that led to a plateau or drop off, to a much more effective steady climb with a steep jump that hopefully peaks right around those playoff games. Every season, that climb builds on itself until the team is consistently becoming greater.

So how does that look, this culture building stuff? It's not a big circle where we sit around and discuss our feelings and I say, 'hey no sticks the first three weeks.' We must still be learning and growing, mastering our craft, playing a sport we love to play, conditioning, and studying. But when the focus is placed on culture, those drills and activities have a slightly different feel. The stress to perfect it right away is gone and the patience of just teaching, trying, asking questions, and getting to know each other's' strengths and weaknesses becomes easier. It's no longer all about that immediate win, it's about the end game. It's about development. It's about building an experience so much greater and yet also going for limitless goals and a vision of accomplishing incredible feats.

As the strength of the players self-belief grows, as the feeling of connectivity between players grows, and the feelings of mastery start to build, the learning capacity begins to grow exponentially. They fear the new information less, trust trying it a little more, get more excited about applying it out on the field, and the communication gets stronger. The trust between players, between players and coaches, and maybe even players, parents, and coaches, has been built. The foundation is there and every piece of information that's built on top of it as the team enters the most important part of the season becomes incredibly powerful.

Try this. Sit in a chair with both feet on the floor. Stand up putting 70 percent or so of your focus and weight in your weaker/non-dominant leg but keep your core straight up so no one can see you are shifting your weight. Essentially you are still standing up, still balanced, still getting it done. But your focus is on building that one leg's strength that has been weak or sometimes even gets neglected. Imagine your focus is on that leg for a few weeks every time you just do what you do all the time, stand up. Now that you've built it up, stand up using both legs equally. You're going to be stronger now that you have both legs working at full capacity and your weak leg has been strengthened.

Here's the thing about our culture that we so often allow to sit. That we usually don't put a primary focus on – think about your legs: Even if you are trying to kick a ball with your dominant and more powerful leg, the weak leg must balance your body and give you stability. If it buckles, the kick will never happen. **STRENGTHEN YOUR WEAK LEG, the one that supports your team, that keeps them going, the one that really all other things stem from, FIRST.**

Put your focus on culture first. Build it, guide it, grow it, and then as they are excited and learning at top capacity with a strong belief system in each other, go and reach new heights!

How Long Does Culture Take to Change?

Culture doesn't change overnight, but a shift in belief, focus, and attitude can be seen in a team as soon as they decide to commit to making it happen.

What can a 45-minute conversation between coaching staff and best-selling Author and speaker Jon Gordon and 20 copies of his book The Energy Bus do for a team on the brink of destruction? I just had the privilege of finding out exactly what can happen and it wasn't a season of gradual change, it was only a week.

A small college team facing undertones of negativity, some that have been building from past seasons, combined with brand new players, two new coaches made a recipe for disaster. With players quitting on a daily basis and others ready to do the same, a phone call to Jon Gordon clarified exactly why the coaching staff needs to set the culture, rather than the staff reacting to a team set culture the whole season.

It went a little something like this...

Day 1 – team is given the Energy Bus books and told that we need to make our culture a priority. Most of the players feeling like they really don't want another book to read... But they (most of them) reluctantly agree to read the first 1/4 of the book. Several eye rolls were spotted...

Day 3 – we meet and discuss the chapters before practice. Some of them have clearly read it and were enthusiastic, some have definitely not even read the first page. No major noticeable changes except a few do participate in the conversation. Still some eye rolling going on from those who didn't read. Practice is still low energy, players still hanging out in small groups rather than all together. Some Negative self-talk still going on.

Day 5 – everyone seems to be reading the book, we are halfway through and more people are joining in the conversation. They are starting to relate the characters in the book to themselves. A vision is created by the players. Practice is still low energy but there is a little less drama going on. Coaches are starting to wonder if this is going to work inside of a week when the tickets will be sent out to get on the bus...but strive to remain positive.

Confessions of an Imperfect Coach

Fast forward to the last day. The team is sent a bus ticket via email and told to sign it and return it to coach's office if they are on the bus. Lots of breath holding and hoping...

Every player turns in a ticket. Tickets are invites for individual players to get on the bus. This is when the magic happened. Practice that night was clearly changed. The atmosphere was light, the players were no longer grouped into cliques, there was encouragement, laughing, and individual skills were even looking better. There was a shift in the atmosphere, in the self-talk, and in the purpose of being there. The talk was about the future rather than complaining of the past or present or about each other.

No, we didn't right the Titanic in a week, but it felt like we patched the holes that were trying to flood our foundation and bring it down. The ship needs to be maintained throughout the season and we have work to do, but we've gotten a hold on the situation.

I know that if we had tried to work on each player individually and not brought our issues out in the open together, it would have taken a lot longer. By bringing the team together, creating a vision, and getting that commitment from them together to get on the bus-make a commitment to each other in writing, make the choice to be positive-we unified a team that appeared to be beyond repair.

At the CORE

I crouched down, one knee buried in the warm turf pellets and the other clasping my oversized white board. A group of teenage girls sat in front of me; dirty, tired, and frustrated. A season long run of victories, excitement, and then injury after injury tugging at our hopeful chances of playing in the top two at the state tournament before us. They had overcome the odds getting their first state birth and executed a virtually undefeated season. They had surprised everyone, surpassed their own expectations, done something incredible.

But there we were. Half time at the semi-final game and I had nothing. Nothing to draw on the board. Nothing to say, no magical speeches, no clue. We weren't playing well. Our young team had to pull this off without their senior leaders who were trying but unable to play through injuries and they were crumbling. We were watching the other team run through us like water through a sieve and they knew it. We scored on ourselves attempting a clear. We ran past ground balls. We dropped everything. We were not the team we had been all season and because I hadn't known that positive culture wasn't just a good thing to have but rather THE most important thing to build, when we were tested with adversity we all sat there pretty much speechless. We had no path built to move us forward, no real connections to rely on.

Are you giving up? Do you want this? Get out there and start playing!

It's to date my worst half time speech. I knew it at the time, I silently prayed for anything better to say, but I had nothing. How do you take a group of defeated players and get them to re-engage in the game, to believe in themselves? I had stopped believing. I didn't see any way we could pull this one out and I was frustrated.

It was a valuable lesson. As I left that game it occurred to me that outside teaching the game, I had no idea what I was doing. None. I spent the next couple of years trying to find ways to motivate players. Contests, prizes, awards, snacks, team building trips, but the culture didn't budge.

I can still feel the frustration. WHAT AM I MISSING?!? Cursing the fact that I'd never had a coach that worked on culture, I

Confessions of an Imperfect Coach

realized that I had no role model to follow. I had no mentor, no way to figure this out -but it wasn't because I didn't care or wasn't trying. I was consumed by the challenge. But the more I tried, the more I felt like I was failing my team. I questioned my ability to be a coach despite my love of teaching the game. Nothing was working and I got more and more bad advice.

Call it divine intervention, call it fate, but I found the piece I was missing through some extraordinary circumstances that came across in God's ever perfect timing. I had been looking at everything backwards. What I had chosen to put as the core of my program (Lax IQ) was surviving and thriving because it was my main focus. The things outlying that core were withering. They weren't being nurtured, implemented, or supported. They were circles outside of my core with no direct connection.

I had been wrong all along when I was trying to solve the problem. I didn't need to learn how to maintain a better team culture that was crumbling half way through the season. Rather it was that I had never built it in the first place. I was allowing the players, parents, misunderstandings, poor communication, circumstances, and disappointments build my team's culture. Most teams are positive at the beginning as the excitement of a new season begins. But each challenge starting with team placement and cuts, added another knot in the cord, another bruise on the surface of the fruits of our labor. I couldn't maintain it because it was completely at the whim of whatever we faced. Injured player? Bad weather? Hostility? Playing time? Difficult refs? Those things owned us, and no amount of telling players to just play through would fix our outlook. The players didn't know what the alternative was, all they knew was to drown in the tides of unfortunate circumstance when things went wrong. Or to live off the highs of short lived victories.

What does this do to a team over the course of a sports season? Players, coaches, and parents begin to need those victories, playing time, and rewards. They crave them, focus on them, need them. Because the uncontrollable events feel so intolerable, the alternative only leaves that quest for immediate gratification to soothe the frustrations.

In this climate, it starts to feel like everything is stacked against you, like no matter what you do something is always stealing your ability to move ahead. Each season felt like the obstacles were just getting bigger and more frequent. It rained more every season. The refs were worse. It was colder. The parents were more difficult. Or were they? We started blaming, complaining. Sometimes even the wins started to lose their luster because the sting of everything else was gripping us so tightly. You know you've hit some sort of crisis when the win lacks joy and has players worried about who played and if the coach said the right thing or not.

Build your core on something controllable, positive, something that you can believe in no matter what storm you stand in the middle of. Your core belief is what will last and thrive, it's what sustains your greatest focus. Then connect every piece of your program to that core with a life line. Check that line frequently for kinks, blocks, and loose ends. Be diligent in the health and vitality of your connections.

There were two events that changed my core beliefs in coaching. One was facing my own mortality after my pulmonary embolism and realizing exactly what still mattered when everything was at stake. The other was meeting an author who filled in the blank for me. When I was silently screaming out to the world "what am I missing," Jon Gordon somehow crossed my path and his books and conversations filled that need for a mentor who understood culture. *The Energy Bus*, Jon's own transformational story, *The Seed, and The carpenter* are where I learned that the core must be planted firmly in positive leadership, love, care, connection, purpose. That no matter the task in life, it must stem from there before it can grow. It's the reason I am so passionate about sharing these ideas and stories to programs today.

This core became love, and it connected to the players, lacrosse, fun, learning through lifelines and daily checks to keep those connections clear. It turned me from a transactional coach to a transformational coach. I'm not just talking about the players. I'm talking about every single person in the program, including myself, growing in a greater purpose through playing and coaching a sport. I'm talking about the lives we touch who come watch us play, who sit on the opposing player sideline, and who interact with us in our daily lives. If you aren't in awe of the opportunity to reach an incredible scope of people in a positive way or conversely to make a negative impact through sports, then take a step back and see the bigger picture. If it's a little overwhelming then you get it, you know this is more than a game.

What's in your core? What is the one most important thing and does everything else have some sort of connection back to the center to keep it going? Don't be me at that silent, frustrated half-time with nothing to say.

Instead tell them – I love you guys. I love being on this field with you as you battle out an incredible challenge. I don't know what's going to happen second half, but I know it will be spectacular because that's what you do best. I know that at the end of this game we are going to huddle up and shout out the best and the bravest moments that you are about to go experience because I know what's in your hearts. I know whatever is coming, we will be better for it.

Then send them out there, core intact, connections in place, and hold on tight.

Culture Shock

I remember vividly taking my first high school head coaching job, all the fears and insecurities about running a team were stressing me out. I look back on what I was worried about the most, now years later, and I see clearly just how much I didn't know, that I just didn't know.

Breaking down skills, teaching the game, making on the fly adjustments, countering the other team's strategies, and creating optimal match ups were a top priority; but a place where I felt at least partially competent or less intimidated to figure out. My biggest worry was the administrative parts that I'd never done before. Organizing our schedule, practice apparel and uniforms, working around spring break, getting the fields lined correctly, having keys to the building on a Saturday when it's locked and not setting off the alarms, having the fields set and broken down on game days, and balancing a budget all the while working with a set of booster parents who didn't know anything about me.

As I began to conquer my fears, as the admin work turned out to be not so big of a deal, and the team was winning and learning at an incredible rate, I felt as though I had figured it all out. I loved my players, loved coaching, and we were moving ahead and growing in skill and number like no one had anticipated.

The funny thing about hindsight is that you recognize the signs later that at the time were so clearly right in front of you. My culture was rotting; but I didn't see it. It was rotting out of sight, behind closed doors, away from my attention, and slow enough that it took a year or two before it was staring me in the face.

Ask me now what my focus is with my teams, what my most important key to success is, what I should have feared from the beginning rather than the details, the admin, the fields, and I will say culture. A team can win and be organized in every way, but come crashing down because the culture is left to form itself. Everything trickles down from culture; the admin, the plans, the strategy, the players, all follow the direction of what philosophy is or isn't built for that program to stand on.

Confessions of an Imperfect Coach

I reached a point in coaching where finally I knew exactly what I didn't know. I didn't know how to build a culture, how to keep drama, hurt feelings, miscommunication, confusion, rumors, and pot stirrers from destroying a team. I knew how to build a team, but I didn't know how to maintain it without it imploding. As GI Joe says, knowing is HALF the battle. It wasn't until I opened a copy of Jon Gordon's bestseller *The Energy Bus* early that year that I fully understood the concept of driving my team's culture and empowering my players to do the same. It wasn't until I understood the concept of energy vampires, team buy-in, filling space with positivity to keep negativity from creeping in. I was missing the very simple but team and life changing concept that as soon as a team of people buy into the value of working together for a greater purpose, a change can occur. That we could start our season already united instead of trying to build unity with wins or reacting to losses.

I never coached the same way again. I never let culture be a byproduct of players emotions or a reaction to misunderstandings; situational in any way, never again. I spent the next couple of years fine tuning my culture-building and figuring out the best way to build both team and parent buy in – it's how I created the concept of Meeting in the Middle for the best program experience.

Jon Gordon and Mike Smith have laid out in detail in *You Win In The Locker Room First,* just how to direct culture so that any kind of team, any group of people under leadership, can thrive beyond the X's and O's. They can thrive beyond the immediate goal of accomplishing a specified task, because they believe in a bigger concept – the absolute success of and collaboration with EACH OTHER.

How do I know it's working? That my teams are stronger and unified because I changed my approach?

- I know because they get better in the second half no matter how tough the first half is – they actually strengthen each other when things get tough instead of falling apart.
- I know because we can have open conversations without defensiveness when we don't immediately see eye to eye leading to greater collaboration.

- I know because more players come back for the experience of being a part of the team over their love of the sport.
- I know because the Energy Vampires are too uncomfortable to stay.

Culture will never take a back seat again, it's going to be up front, shot gun, right next to us drivers deciding exactly where we will take it.

Are You Trying to SELL Culture?

If someone is telling you they experienced incredible results, and then tells you that it was easy, they are about to sell you something.

That's because results take consistent work over time, including days you don't want to. Including the days you don't feel well, or are super busy, or are stressed out, sore, tired, or don't feel motivated.

Are you trying to sell your team on culture? Have you become more of a salesman desperate for that buy-in than a coach or a leader? This is a trap that rarely ends well. Are you promising results, promising a family-like atmosphere, promising unity, promising this will be a fantastic season – all things you could never guarantee? Are you just telling your team and your parents that this is how it is and expecting it to be so, perhaps blaming them for falling short if they don't simply comply with your description of team utopia? These are all things that you can't hand them, that they must help build.

Leaders don't stand on the sideline directing traffic, they are inside the car with their team – alongside them, asking the players to drive while they instruct, correct, and encourage. That's how you build consistency. That's how you build buy-in. That's how you shape culture. Day by day, interaction by interaction.

It's day in and day out belief in your athletes. Belief in their potential. Belief in a future that can survive whatever is coming your way. Believing it when you can't see it, when you are certain it's not within your reach but you carry on, move forward, and you build it imperfect brick by imperfect brick.

When that preseason talk comes around, don't sell them on how the culture is going to be and beg for a buy-in without any work being put in. Instead, tell your players that it's going to be hard, dirty, uncomfortable, tedious, and stressful work. It's going to be fun, exciting, rewarding, memory and lifetime friendship building and character growing too. But sometimes it will be frustrating, empty, confusing, and you're going to experience a game or a practice when you just might think it's not worth it. That's when we build our culture, that's where our relationships get stronger, that's where we find out the true meaning of seeing something through until you find success, that's where you get your return on the time and money you put into sports. I'm looking forward to battling the elements of the season with you, alongside you, out in front of you, bringing in the anchor, and helping you navigate through it all. This will be our culture, no promises, no sales, just us, committed to seeing this thing through, and whatever lies ahead. Our adventure awaits.

On a Collision Course or On a Mission?

Get on the same tracks, climb aboard the train, get on the same path. It's what we've all been working towards with our teams. If we're going to the same place then we can be united, right? But as I sat in a cab in New York City this afternoon, on a one-way road, I realized that the same direction isn't enough. As other cabs, bicycles, pedestrians, and drivers navigated the same road at different speeds and with different characteristics, each one was focused only on their own journey. Every time there was a pot hole or obstruction, a collision almost occurred. These different vehicles had a common destination, Point A to Point B, but everyone was in it for themselves.

Teams can be riding towards a common goal, perhaps a championship game, a milestone, a record something or other. But if each person has their own best interest out in front, the team will still be tripping over each other, crashing around obstacles, and colliding as they go along. Getting on the same road is a start, but your team can still crash and burn.

How can you make sure your team is sharing the journey, using each other's abilities as strengths, and avoiding collisions? You can't just have a common goal. You can't just name the road and go as fast and hard as you can.

Your team must be on a mission together. Every Day. Every Practice. With Intention.

1. Build a TEAM first mentality. Everyone loves stats, but consider focusing on team stats as a whole and trying together to bring up weak spots or celebrate strengths.
2. Make decisions as a team. Our team either wears their cold gear as a team to match, or no one wears it. A small, seemingly worthless decision, but they are learning to compromise, do things for the team as a whole and not always put themselves first.
3. Encourage a giving, thankful, environment that openly praises, lifts up, and celebrates each other. Awkward as it may feel at first, this atmosphere usually builds upon itself easily as soon as it becomes an accepted practice.

4. Never leave a player behind. It may feel easier to write off that player that isn't pulling their weight, but for the good of the team and the benefit of valuing every player, go back and run that player to the finish line, challenge them to step up, or pair them up for more instruction. Get them back on track.

5. Make sure players know their roles so they aren't colliding and tripping over each other. Competition is ok, that's why we have passing lanes. But cutting each other off and slamming into other roles isn't going to end well. What's your role, and what's the path to changing or improving that role? How can you assist those around you? How can you all get safely to the destination and celebrate reaching that goal at the end? Can you all see the vision clearly?

Don't just get on the same road with your teammates, avoid the collision and get on a mission!

Build a Limitless Team

What is it, really, that is so important about having coaches? Certainly, in the future we could replace our flawed, fully human, and mistake-bound selves with robots that have more knowledge than I'll ever have. There's no shortage of how-to info or even easy access to it out there these days. So, what's really the most important thing I can provide as a coach that they can't get online, at a camp, or by reading?

Connection. The most important asset a coach has for their players is the human connection. I can give them my belief in them, my care and concern for them, my understanding, my patience, my guidance, my accountability, my feedback, and my adjustments to their feedback that make me a better coach.

And what can we do with that connection? Guide them to find out they are more than they knew they could be. Not just by teaching them more skills or pushing them harder. But by the sheer power of that connection, that belief in them.

Humans come into everything they do with self-imposed limits. We all have a roof. Some have a relatively high roof, with goals under it that they feel are reachable. Others are being crushed by a short roof that feels like they've already capped out their talent, that growth is unlikely. That roof has risen and lowered with their own confidence level; but it's always there. Whatever height roof they come in with, my job is to show them how to rip it off, and remove the ceiling altogether. To show them that there are no real limits.

I want them to do something that's outside of and above the roof they've built. Something that challenges themselves to do exactly what they believe they cannot do. That they thought only others could accomplish. To have the courage to step onto a new path knowing they will likely fall down just to teach themselves that they can get back up and keep going. That drive and persistence can erase those self-made boundaries and thoughts. They can expand growth potential beyond their own comprehension and think bigger, wider, and deeper than before.

How can I do something I don't believe I can do? How can my growth not only impact my sport, but my life, and even the lives of those around me? What if I'm stronger than I thought I was?

What if my teammates are struggling with the same ceiling, and what happens when we break through it together?

What kind of player does a coach need on a team that is multi-dimensional and has limitless potential? How do we manage team selections with that in mind? A coach needs players with heart, desire, the will to learn, the courage to step outside the lines and try something different, the tenacity to get back up, and embrace failure. A coach needs players who will trust in and believe in their teammates – even when those teammates fail and let them down because we've committed to allowing mistakes to sharpen us. A coach needs players who will trust in and believe in their coaches – even when those coaches fail and let them down, because at times, despite being on the same path and wanting the best for their players, coaches do, in fact, also step out on a limb, fail, and let players down.

A coach and the players need parents who are ready to jump into a limitless future for their daughters and sons. Parents who agree to not allow talk in front of, or to, their child about blame, comparison, and doubt. Who avoid the *would have-could have-should have* conversations. Parents who celebrate the learning opportunities with discussions that let the player talk about those mistakes and how they would approach it next time, letting the player talk through and walk through this journey with full support in their own learning process. A coach and players need parents who realize that connection is the most important thing, and that when a disconnect and misunderstandings start to form, a reconnect is a priority before anyone loses sight of the goals or starts rebuilding those limits once again.

Who does this team need to come out and play? Everyone who wants to be a part of it. Every person who loves this sport, who wants to be a part of an adventure- because that's what stepping outside of comfort zones and blasting through ceilings really is. Every player has a role, and every role has a value that makes a team and a season what it is. You may not know that role yet, and even as you step into the season your role may change – maybe even more than once. But each player fills a piece of a puzzle that would lay empty without them. All of the greatest athletes in the world cannot make a well-rounded, inspired, limit destroying team if they don't have the right personalities to build something of real value. If you want to be a part of something, part of a group that's about to test the limits and then free themselves of those limits; then this is probably just what you're looking for. Start making your list. What can you accomplish that you never thought you could? What lives can we touch and make better through our own sports experience; how can this be so much bigger than us?

The adventure is coming. The inside jokes, the new ideas, the tried and true favorites, the traditions, the new traditions, the struggles, the connections, friendships, and the realization that YOU can be and do whatever it is that you believe you can be and do. **Every learning opportunity is a new adventure if we always choose to see it as a door opening.** That path didn't work? Thank you for trying and showing us that we need to open a new door. Where shall we go next?

Losing? It's Not Them; It's You.

Is your team struggling? Have you had rough season after rough season and they aren't getting better? Are you studying the game and throwing out new drills but still chasing the W?

Lacrosse is full of technical, mechanical, strategic concepts, and rules. It's a hard game to teach. But here's the bottom line. If your team was driven, motivated, united, and hungry; they would eventually find a way to put that little ball into their opponents net if they have even a little bit of knowledge about the game.

Everyone has a bad season or a rebuilding year or two. But if you're on year 3 or 4 of misery, then it's not skills or your players that are failing you.

Here's what you don't want to hear. It's not the team. It's not your lacrosse knowledge. It's not because they didn't work hard enough in the off season. If you're struggling year after year, I have news for you... you don't hold the market on entitled teens. You don't have more difficult parents than the rest of the world. Your players aren't less athletic. Believe me, no one can avoid the array of personalities and athletic abilities that come with every team.

It's your coaching.

"Wait!" You say. "I tell them that we're a family. I tell them to play together, to get along, to work harder. To focus, to practice more. They just don't listen!"

You can't tell your team to have great culture, to battle 'til the sound of every whistle and every horn. To leave their hearts and souls on the field and to love each other as teammates. You can't tell them to want to work in the off season or come to practice excited to learn and appreciate being pushed when they are tired. You can't tell parents to support you, to be positive, to cause less drama.

You can't tell them to do it, *you must build it*. Even though I see it every year. The coach emails everyone stating that the team will act as a family and there will be no conflict. Good luck with that! That doesn't work. You must make a culture that allows that to form. You must create and nourish an environment where greatness takes root and thrives.

Confessions of an Imperfect Coach

How? I thought you'd never ask:

1. Create an environment where trying new things and attempting to improve on weaknesses is not only safe, it's celebrated. Consistently. We are often good at this sometimes, but then forget when important games are on the line.
2. Replace pointing out mistakes with pointing out victories. Write the mistakes into your practice plan by creating drills to work on those skills. Give specific instruction – keep your head up, get lower, etc. But make the correction in no more than one sentence and keep your body language patient and relaxed.
3. Facilitate 'getting to know each other better' activities on a regular basis. I love Jon Gordon's hot seat where players share a hero, hardship, and highlight moment.
4. Take an interest in each player beyond their ability to play the game. Show them their value is beyond their performance so they don't get hung up on a bad game or performance.
5. Give hand written encouragement notes to at least 2 players a week. Encourage them to do the same for each other.
6. Celebrate every victory. No matter how small.
7. Let them think for themselves. Avoid the over coaching, over talking, over game scripting and allow their minds to read and adjust to situations.
8. Ask them how they could fix it before trying to tell them how. It builds confidence.
9. Assure your parents through any conflict just how much you value their child and offer positive feedback on what they are doing well.
10. Bring a positive outlook and a smile. Your players are a reflection of you.
11. Read up on culture building, mindset development, and positive coaching! It's game changing!

You want to become the powerhouse you think your players can never become? Build a unified, driven, caring, and safe atmosphere and watch their unmet potential become reality.

All-In Starts with You, Coach

Loyalty, All-In, Family. Just a few of the key words we use as coaches to promote an atmosphere of driving with purpose towards a common goal. We often talk to our players about loyalty to their teammates and the mission. We press them to be all-in, not just giving a part of themselves out there every day, but to commit to putting out their best efforts even on the tough days. We talk about family, about how even if we don't necessarily get along all the time, we always have each other's backs and best interests at heart.

But there are teams who have mastered this kind of culture, and others who just preach it to no avail. What gives?

All In, loyalty, and family come from the top down. I've seen teams that start strong with these concepts as they are promised from their leadership only to fade out and crumble throughout the season. It's time to ask ourselves as coaches, are WE all in? Do WE have their backs? How about those days when they aren't playing well, are less focused, what if they are falling behind? Do we jump our attention over to the ones getting it done, do we threaten, or act in ways that make our players wonder if they might not have value anymore? Or are we all-in for ALL of the players we have chosen to be on our teams, no matter what?

What if we are having an off day, feeling stressed, frustrated? Do we push that aside and focus the way we ask them too, or is it an excuse to be a little harsher at practice or maybe even a little complacent? I heard of a coach that actually sat on the bench through practice letting the captains run it because he was 'emotionally drained' that day. What kind of example does that set for work ethic? How often are our players emotionally drained from their crazy schedules, yet we ask them to put that aside and do work at the same level; are we doing that? Are we giving what we are asking for in return at the same level of commitment?

Are we rallying for them when then need it, or leaving them behind? Are we loyal to our players in the same way we ask them to be loyal to the team, or do we trade them around with our loyalty given to the wins, points, and titles they can bring us?

Because they know; our players know what we value deep down, and it matters a great deal to the culture we are building.

When we are leading people to a goal, the people must come first. And when we put our people first, they will reach that goal. Loyalty, faith, and trust in our players are the only things that builds loyalty, faith, and trust in our teams. Fear and uncertainty build only more Fear.

Some of the greatest coaches, who teach accountability and have the highest standards, have incredible culture because they are ALL-IN for every player on their team. They can push a little harder, because their players know that if they fail, if they have a bad day, the coach isn't going to write them off, but rather step in to redirect, care about them and help them get where they need to go. Players are part of the team, they don't play in fear of losing that. If a player falls behind, they will catch back up on the sheer belief they know in their heart that their coach has in them and the fact that their coach won't quit on them, ever. That kind of devotion from a coach is what builds the all-in atmosphere. Not that twitter hashtag, not the word you have screen printed on the back of the players shooters, not the speeches about how they aren't living up to that family, loyalty, all-in theme for the season. They will return in great number what attitude and focus their coach consistently puts out, and nothing else.

A coach who is all-in for every player, in all circumstances, builds a culture that can claw its way through any challenge, any adversity, because they know the leader isn't going to let anyone get left behind.

All-In starts with you coach, then you can set the expectation and they will follow your lead.

Confessions of an Imperfect Coach

Team Inspiration

For your players motivation and
accountability

Team 8. Play for More.

I've been to enough club tournaments that I expect the expected. Screaming coaches. Parents yelling at the refs. Trash talking between players, often mismatched in size. Parents in the stands cheering, parents leaning over the fence yelling not quite as cheerfully. Cranky officials who haven't had a break in hours melting in the heat. As a career coach, former player, and a sports parent, I'm rarely surprised by anything anymore. But at my son's first tournament of the summer last weekend, I was reminded that inspiration and humanity rest around every corner, if only we open our eyes to see it.

With all the usual weekend game madness going on, the focus was on the typical drama all around me, and how my son personally was performing or if he was having fun. I hardly noticed a team all in orange and blue that I passed by several times without a second thought. But between games I overheard a conversation about that orange and blue team, about Team 8.

That's an intriguing name, I thought. I've seen some creative names at summer ball, but something drew me in to ask what this 8 was all about. As I walked over towards their players resting between games, I saw their tent with a banner hanging across it that read 'Live for Jamie.' A single blue jersey with the number 8 hung from the inside of the tent. As I scanned the players I realized that every single player in orange and blue had an 8 in their number. But no one wore the number 8 by itself, only the lone blue jersey held that honor.

It was in the following moments that I found myself wresting with completely different emotions than the typical ones I face at tournaments. Usually I deal with exhaustion, frustration, excitement and even more often-disgust at the whole scene. But as the mother and father of Jamie told me what this team was about, my motherly heart broke and then filled back up with an incredible love of what the lacrosse community stands for, and how it does amazing things when a tragedy strikes.

In 2013, Jamie McHenry, a powerful shooter and well-loved middle school attack player nicknamed 'Rocket Shot,' was on spring break with friends in Florida. He was struck and killed by a car while crossing a busy street. A young life gone in the blink of an eye, a player who had picked up his stick with his teammates for the last time.

Jamie's love of the sport of lacrosse, and a mission to keep his spirit alive from his family and friends lead to the creation of Team 8 and the Live for Jamie Foundation. This team plays in Jamie's memory and they all wear his # 8 incorporated into their number. They bring his number 8 jersey to each tournament and hang it up.

I watched Team 8 play. I watched them honor the game of lacrosse. I felt the love they had for their lost teammate, and I saw the pride they took in carrying on their friend's legacy. I watched them win, play with sportsmanship, with teamwork and skill. I watched Jamie's parents cheer this team on as though all of the players were a part of their family.

I felt something incredibly powerful stir inside me watching a team playing for something so much bigger and so much more meaningful than a tournament trophy or stats. Everything changes when we play for a cause; especially one that's meant to uplift and honor. It really could change this game, our sports culture that's currently rotting, if we all found a greater purpose in our competition and our coaching.

A little hesitant to bother a group of teenage boys, I asked for a picture. These were some of the kindest kids you could ask to meet on a tournament field, and they were honored to show what their team was all about. This, I thought, is what is missing on so many of our fields; purpose, a bigger cause.

The Live for Jamie Foundation creates scholarship opportunities for young lacrosse players. Team 8 creates an opportunity for lacrosse players and athletes of all sports to be inspired when we hear their story to step outside of the travel-scholarship-money triangle and represent something that means so much more. What do you play for? What do you coach for? At the end of the summer, of your career, did it mean something – did it change something for the better? Did you honor anyone – did you honor yourself?

Thank you, Team 8, for reminding me what our community, and our young athletes are capable of. For being open to share your story with me and pose for pictures. As I watched my son's team play on the adjacent field, I kept close to my heart that this game means more than the tournament atmosphere presents, that there's a very real and valuable reason we are trying so hard to save youth sports.

We have forgotten, because we've been sucked into a whirlwind sports culture that idolizes self-centered accolades, that a greater purpose is still there, hiding in the shadows. Instead of walking past the team 8's around us, more concerned with what team is in the playoff bracket for the trophy, who our refs will be, or who has the best uniforms, we need to stop and get to know the stories and people around us, make our own stories, find our purpose, and play bigger.

What do you play for?

Learn more about Jamie's Story, Team 8 and the Live for Jamie Foundation:

www.liveforjamie.com

Mistakes Lead to Greatness

Turning a quitting mentality into greatness: How much of an edge would we have over other teams if our team could bounce back from anything, love learning, always be focused on positivity and building together?

The old *tough love* approach to coaching is at the forefront of our youth participation decline. That drive we must make them better by focusing on, calling out, and shaming mistakes may in fact, be driving them into a pit of hopelessness. I learned this first hand, I used to be a coach that prided myself on corrections and the pursuit of perfectionism. And what I had at the end of all that was a very talented, skilled team of girls that couldn't wait to quit because they felt inadequate. Kids learn mistakes; that's how every day will look to them – mistakes and lessons over and over until they become (hopefully) well rounded adults with life and mistake recovery experience. How often do we forget that it's our job to help them seek answers, different perspectives, and to help them grow?

Failure and *Growth* *look the same. They both are uncomfortable, involve mistakes, falling short of our goal. But one leads to* **quitting***, the other leads to* **greatness***. What kind of athletes do you want?*

What perspective do we offer our athletes when they fall short? Are we pointing out the mistake, calling attention to where it went wrong and leaving the attention there? Are they leaving that interaction or that mistake feeling defeated and inadequate? Does it make them want to give up? Did we even address it at all? Growing hurts, it feels the same sting of failure. But with the right leadership, that failure can shift into motivation, or conversely it can tear them apart and drain their confidence and future performances.

Depending on their perception of mistakes, a player can either hang their head or dig deep and become more skilled. **Two very different outcomes from the same situation and we have the ability, as coaches, to shape that perception. Pretty amazing! And how often we forget to use that responsibly...**

How do we turn failure, the feeling of hopelessness, into a feeling of empowerment, motivation and learning? *Celebrate*

Confessions of an Imperfect Coach

mistakes instead of punishing them. Ouch, hard to do! They messed up, we practiced it over and over and they get on the field and do it wrong! Incredibly frustrating, but not just for us coaches. They are likely frustrated with themselves as well, we must keep steering them in the right direction until they can do it on their own and then, and only then is our job done. They will beat themselves up over it, our job if we want strong teams with motivated players, is to empower and lead; not to judge or punish.

Opportunities to turn a Failure Perspective into a Growth Perspective – Turn a quitting mentality into greatness:

Pre-Practice Talk: These are the skills we are working on today. Think about what you personally need to focus on the most and think about that every time it's your turn to go. Report back to me at the end of practice any improvements you notice in yourself and your teammates. Don't forget to call out improvements you see in your teammates as we practice today as well.

Post-Practice talk: Who messed up today? Tell us about it and then tell us one important lesson you learned from it that you will apply tomorrow.

Pre-Game Talk: What lessons did you apply at practice this week that will help you today? What are our strengths and how can we use them together to be as strong as possible? What would you like to focus on the first half? What are our advantages as a team?

Half-time Talk: What opportunities do you see to improve the second half – what can we do better? What are we doing really well that we should continue (no matter how small)? Who has more energy they can throw on the fire to bring up the heat? Where is the other team struggling and how can we use our strengths to combat them?

Post-Game Talk: (regardless of a win or loss) Where did we excel? Who made a mistake and then made a correction before the game was over? Did we make any mistakes where we don't know how to fix them? What do you think we did the best, and where do you need more help at next week's practices? Whose fire burned brightest – who gave the most effort today?

Build a team that grows through adversity instead of crumbles. Build players that are mentally tough, think about how to get better and who have a strong growth mentality. Coaches have an incredible opportunity to shift mind sets, perspective, and provide the tools these kids will use for success far beyond sports. At the end of the season, what will they take away from your leadership focus?

It's our kids jobs to try over and over again and to make mistakes so they can learn what works and what doesn't. If we go into coaching with the mindset that these players are here to make mistakes, and that we are here to help them recover from those mistakes, then frustration goes significantly down and our focus can be on building mentally strong and prepared athletes.

Show up. Work hard. Be nice.

Want to be the best? How about the coach's favorite? Want playing time? Let's keep this simple. Focus on the things you can control and do them with intention every day, consistently. There's no secret formula to success, it is what it always has been, and it happens to be a matter of choice.

Show up. Work hard. Be nice.

Show up. Physically be there, that's number one. Stop over scheduling your commitments and start honoring them instead. That may mean sacrifice. It's time to go all-in. Be ready to go at start time, not pulling up. If you're late, hustle onto the field, show you care about not wasting valuable training time. Be present mentally, tune out the rest of the day, listen to learn, and ask questions. Avoid being a distraction, add value to the practice.

Work hard. You may not be the best skilled, but you can always be the hardest worker. Don't get sweaty just because you're running sprints, get sweaty in all the drills. Raise the level of competition, raise the bar. No matter what's happening, working as hard as you are able is always an option.

Be nice. Respecting teammates, coaches, parents, people at school, and being kind is a win win for everyone. Mean people will be there no matter what, your kind influence will either help or have no impact, but returning negativity will guarantee to pull you and your teammates down. Encourage, assist, try to see another point of view, and let go of things that aren't going to affect the big picture. Don't engage in teasing, or talking about teammates or coaches behind their backs, walk away or better yet, steer the conversation in a positive direction instead.

Your team's success on the field relies on a solid, positive culture and you as a team member must own your part in that.

Have a great season!

Get Used to Disappointment

What will your epitaph say? How about, "she finished everything." Doesn't quite have that accomplished ring to it, does it? Yet our society, with participation medals for just about anything, has gotten to a place where finishing is enough. If you didn't quit, then you have succeeded. Our kids are losing the drive to reach their potential, and we're feeding them the lie that life is too hard to compete so just get through it, get your medal and celebrate not quitting.

When did disappointment and falling short of a goal become so cruel and life shattering that we felt we needed to stop competing out of fear of failure? Failure is a catalyst, as it drives success by pushing people to work harder and outside of their comfort zone. When we take the opportunity for failure away from our kids and from ourselves, we must replace it with something; which is usually complacency and acceptance of mediocrity in reaching their own personal best.

We all have great intentions to protect our kids from what some of us experienced when we faced failure. But we have gotten the message wrong -without protecting them at all. No one wants a kid to feel like they aren't performing the way they should, or to be hurt and feel defeated. So, we took away the only hope they had to improve by removing competition. Instead of empowering these kids with a thought process that; they have control over their performance through hard work, focus, resiliency, and confidence, we have instead told them that they are all the same and that effort doesn't matter as long as you finish. As long as you don't quit.

Anigo Montoya received the best advice for all of us from the man in black in The Princess Bride, "get used to disappointment." We can't remove disappointment from life; sports used to be one of the best ways to learn how to face disappointment and use it to strive to be better. We've created a world of black and white for our kids, where they either aren't good enough, and never will be, so we eliminate an activity (or coach) that might disappoint them; or we tell them they are all the same and they get an award for not quitting at the end of the season.

Confessions of an Imperfect Coach

Being cut as a freshman from the lacrosse team was the single best motivator I had to get better. I spent every day in the gym, played wall ball until my arms were numb. I had one ball and the wall faced the woods. I knew if I didn't catch it I might lose the ball, I didn't let that ball get by me very often. It drove me to make the team the next year, and had I made the team the first time, I likely wouldn't have put that time in to improve. When I made the team, I knew I had earned it and it felt amazing. If they hadn't cut me, would I have been so driven? Would I have felt as fulfilled at making a team I wasn't ready to be on? Would a participation medal at the end have felt as sweet as that Severna Park Lacrosse Jacket I had earned the right to wear through hard work?

Failure is the catalyst to success. I want to play a game against a team that on paper should just run right through us. It gives us something to improve for, it helps us see where our weaknesses are, and it teaches us that we still have work to do.

How can we then keep our kids from becoming discouraged when they fail, to help build their resiliency, without taking away competition, awards, tryouts, and the opportunity to fail?

The answer lies inside the growth mindset. The ability to believe and have the confidence that they can improve, having a reward for trying to improve, and a focus coming from their coach that effort and mastery is the ultimate measure of success – instead of just finishing.

The next one is a little bit harder because as coaches, we want to win. Allow a defeat to teach how to improve instead of what often becomes shaming, blaming, and being angry for falling short. A loss is an opportunity, and as soon as the team, parents, and coaches see that opportunity clearly, the pressure of winning every game softens and the game becomes what it was meant to be for student athletes; a game. The fear of disappointment can dissipate and in its place is the drive to put your best out there every time, knowing that there's a harness holding you in if you do it wrong, because you're still training safely for life.

A shift in mindset must be clear, concise, and consistent from the coaching staff. It's even more powerful if the parents are on board.

What can I do better? replaces *what did I do wrong?*

How can I train to improve? replaces *why am I not good enough?*

Who can I help get better so that we are better as a team? replaces *why is that other player failing us?*

Talk about how a player can reach their potential. Give them the tools to build the belief that they all have potential. This should replace any conversations about blame –blame the coach, the officials, the other players, the field conditions, the lack of sleep etc.

And what if you put everything out there and you still fail? That's a real possibility, and not just in the world of athletics. It's not a curse to fail, it's a gift and needs to be used, directed into positive channels, and respected. As coaches, we are teaching these kids what the measure of success is. If we define it in points and stats and forget to reward or acknowledge the improvement and work they have put in, then we are asking for a group of finishers instead of achievers. They can't possibly succeed in a realm of uncontrollables. But if instead, the measure of success is everyone's personal best, then failure doesn't feel like failure. It feels more like being outmatched by a worthy opponent. It feels like drive to improve for next time, it feels like burning for a rematch instead of blaming, anger, and quitting.

So your team lost, so you got cut, so you didn't start the last game, now what? Well, what do you want to work on first? Use the gift of failure to find mastery, to reach higher than you thought you could. Let's not take away this valuable tool from our kids by evening the playing field all the time. We need to allow them the opportunity to fail while also giving them the tools to have dignity and hope for growth right alongside it.

Confessions of an Imperfect Coach

My Team is a Wolf Pack

It may be a Wednesday comeback in the middle of a thunderstorm, dashing through raindrops and sliding across plastic grass and ground up tire pellets. It may be a Saturday, sunny, warm, and full of scoring, rising to the occasion, moving the ball brilliantly at times, and sometimes forgetting everything.

Perhaps you see us at a season opener that tests us, shows us where we need to go, checks if we have what it takes to push forward. It could even be a Friday yoga session, where we don't do any real yoga at all, but still leave feeling better and recovered from a hard week.

Maybe you've seen us at practice. Alternating between breaking through new ideas, attempting impossible feats, and spontaneous off-topic and totally distracting conversations and laughter. We played for Patrick (13 year old hockey player at our school that died suddenly of cardiac arrest from an undiagnosed heart defect), we played for our youth players, we played to prove something, we played for each other. We've shared the struggle to learn hard concepts, to execute them, to perfect them when the frustration seemed impossible to get through. We shared the excitement of watching some of those attempts end in perfection. We carried each other on our backs to the goal at practice, literally.

My team is a Wolf Pack. Each individual brings something incredibly important, different perspectives, strengths, personalities, each adding a dimension to the team. Each player brings strengths and faults, strengths that we can build on, faults that we can love and learn from. The pieces may not always appear to fit together, but when this team is on a mission, every part of this pack starts heading in the same direction with a fire in their soul and a mission in their heart...and suddenly this team becomes one incredible force.

My team is a Wolf Pack. Every player has something in their heart that drives them forward. Even as they play to win, play to become their best, they still reach out to bring their teammates with them to the top They stop to pull up the fallen ones, and push and drive on the ones out in front while cheering them on.

One or two players can be strong, they can lead and try to do it on their own. Other teams have strong players and they may go very far relying on them. But there is no stopping a Pack. There is no bringing down a team that has the momentum of a mission driving them on. How can you stop a pack that can withstand falling only to rise stronger, faster, better, and more determined each time? There is no breaking an unbreakable bond, a resolve to keep this team moving forward in one piece to the end of the season.

There is no LIMIT to where a wolf pack goes because there are no barriers that can hold them and no doubts that can drown out their drive to persevere through any situation.

My team is a Wolf Pack, and we've only just begun.

The Path to Greatness

Ever wonder why other people seem to get the opportunities? Other teams, other programs, other players, other coaches, other people seem to reach new heights and you're grinding away waiting for that big break – but it's not coming? Are you still tethered to your comfort zone? Have you changed the story your adversity is telling you? Are you still holding on to something that won't let you break free? Did you know that the harder you must fight to overcome your circumstance, the greater your opportunity to make something amazing out of it becomes? That your struggles may help you, prepare you, mold you and force you to seek something so much bigger in your life? Yes, that difficult team, season, gut wrenching political nightmare, or obstacle may be getting you ready to transform in a major way, if you just let it.

If I hadn't ever stared death in the face, I would have put off so many things that I now seek with passion every single day. Not just my dreams for accomplishments, but my faith, my family, my desire to create positive experiences for my players, and how I take care of myself. If I hadn't had some pretty hard experiences coaching, I'd be a different coach today, a very different coach.

If I had remained comfortable, I would have stayed in that safe environment hoping things would come to me, like making a wish, but not too concerned if they didn't. I'd still be letting my circumstances determine my path, believing I was powerless to change them. I'd believe that I just wasn't lucky, or wasn't able to do anything else. I would be missing out on some of the experiences, relationships, and lessons that I now consider to be some of the greatest in my life. I'd still be falling down a spiral of complacency that led me to put out half-effort, push when it wasn't that hard to push, and fall back into safety when I needed too. Never really getting anywhere, never really feeling brave enough to stand up for what I knew deep inside was important because it was hard, being too concerned with people liking me or agreeing with me, and feeling unfulfilled in my daily tasks because they didn't mean anything.

Where are you in this picture? What can you use to drive you to Greatness and towards your purpose in the short time we have here on this crazy planet? ☺

Finding the opportunities that lead to Greatness

Where Greatness is.

It requires a journey that lies far beyond the comfort zone. Opportunities bring you to greatness. Opportunities are built through adversity. Adversity forces you to leave your comfort zone. Your choices, based on how you interpret your adversity, determine where you go from there.

Where people "think" opportunities are. Feels safe because you're just a step away from that comfort zone. Feels sustainable when there are no major obstacles to face. People use this in their sales tactics (easy results, low risk)

COMFORT ZONE

QUIT ZONE

Uncomfortable, but not willing to cut the string from the comfort zone. Trying to be brave AND comfortable but end up being neither. This is where most people give up. Not getting to their vision, not seeing progress, AND

Most people who have achieved amazing things will tell you that their greatest opportunities came from their most difficult struggles. But we often miss those opportunities because they don't come in the packages we think they do. It probably won't be that perfect offer, phone call, check, intervention that you may be waiting for. Instead, opportunity comes disguised as adversity. They are usually about OTHER people, BIGGER purposes than our desires, and aren't just about US. They aren't put together, clearly outlined or come with instructions. They may be on a different path than you think. Opportunities are built from the daily messages, interactions, connections, and decisions that we make.

Let your uncomfortable, messy, imperfect situation drive you towards something bigger. Something Greater. A vision that's around the corner, that forces you to leave the line of sight of whatever is holding you back from your bigger purpose.

My Team is an Iceberg

The last game of my first season with the Rams is tonight. This has been a different kind of season. It wasn't packed with winning streaks, incredulous score turn-arounds, or even record-breaking accomplishments. We practiced on a small oddly shaped patch of muddy grass that didn't even fit a third of standard size game field, that I lovingly refer to as the goose outhouse. The previous year's my shoes were full of turf pellets, this year it was something a little ickier.

This season held no glamour, no outpouring of love from the media, no unexpected awards. We had small numbers of players, injuries, illnesses, weather, AP tests, field trips – all the usual season challenges of a spring sport.

If I was to use the standard measure of a high school season, I might look back and think we failed, or that at best, we merely got through it. But that's not even close to the reality of Grayson Lacrosse this year. You cannot use a standard measure to define an extraordinary team of young women.

My team is an iceberg. The world may look at the surface and see a small mountain of ice peeking up through the sea, but what we are building is below the surface; a foundation so strong and so massive that all future teams that build upon it will have the opportunity to reach new heights.

A team built around one or two talented players has no foundation. When the peak melts, or when those players leave the program or get injured, there is nothing left to hold that team afloat. Building from the bottom up is the only way to sustain a program and we did that this year. We don't have one or two players who run the game, we have an entire program of players that could, at this very moment, turn around and teach this game inside out because they learned it, studied it, and they know how to sustain, adapt, and build on it.

We all want to hold up the trophy at the end, get the ring, hang the banner, but that comes from building the foundation first-it's what we do that no one can see that propels us into success later. It's the work we do in the dark that one day will shine in the light and will look like an overnight success.

How will you measure this season, what did you build, what will be left next year if your graduating class is large? How would you measure your work in the dark and what will be revealed in the light of the future?

My team is an iceberg. You better put up a lookout.

Perspective Is Everything

My family played a lot of Boggle™ growing up. We still do. I feel like my vocabulary should be better, but I did pretty well just concentrating on small words and then doubling my score by making everything plural. I don't want to brag, but I know a lot of four letter words! (also, three and five letter words…)

If you've never played Boggle, it's a game with large dice that have letters on them and they sit in a grid-like tray. You put the top on the tray and shake it up, making an awful racket, and then you must sit and stare at it for a minute writing down as many words as you can from the displayed letters. Sometimes there were rounds where there was only one vowel and the consonants were made up of Z's, X's, and Q's. Those were tough! Sitting there, pen poised over your blank piece of paper and finding absolutely nothing to write down.

Some rounds would start off well, but then it seemed like all the words were found and there you are, sitting there – chewing on your pen and sweating out the draining plastic sand timer.

The funny thing about Boggle is that you can stare at those letters and think as hard as you want and find nothing, but then spin the tray around so you see it in from another viewpoint, and suddenly words are jumping out so fast you can't write them all down before time runs out.

Perspective Is Everything.

Life is a giant Boggle game. Sometimes you shake it up and all you get are Z's and Q's and you think – what am I going to do with this? It's impossible! Sometimes you feel a rush of opportunity that excites you for the future – all those words right there out in front! and then suddenly they all drop off and then…nothing. Nothing at all.

Even worse, you can sit there writing nothing and notice that the person next to you has a list a page long. Nothing blocks your brain from finding words not finding your purpose faster than suddenly comparing yourself to the person nearest you!

You can sit and stare at the letters and wait for something to change, or you can spin the tray. How often have you waited for an opportunity, or for someone else to make a move, or for the person you're frustrated with to come to you and explain themselves? How often do we use the excuse of being stuck as a safe place? How often do we allow ourselves to sit in negativity, complaining or feeling hopeless – completely blocking out our ability to see the positive side of things?

Spin. The. Tray.

I catch myself as a parent, coach, wife, leader, writer, or speaker feeling like I don't particularly care for the view from where I am. Maybe I'm not succeeding or accomplishing what I think I should be. Perhaps I'm not happy with whatever my current situation is. But I'm either waiting for things to change first, so that I can act or I'm too focused on what I don't like to see anything else. Everyday I'm reminded by the events and experiences of people around me that my perspective can be drastically changed in an instant just by making the choice to see it in another light or truly realize what's important and valuable.

I control the tray – aka my perspective. I don't control what's put in my tray but I can turn it and see it from every angle.

I control how I approach things-what I can give, and what I can try to learn from them. And when I've come at it from every angle – it's time to shake up those letters and look again.

Boggle, er I mean, Play On!!

The Life Ruiner

Many years ago, when I was just starting out as a high school coach, one of my former players tweeted that I was a "life ruiner." It was like a punch in the gut. We'd just come off of a winning season, unquestionably the best season this program had ever had. I'd just been awarded the state high school league's Head Coach of the Year Award.

But in the eyes of this player, I was a life ruiner. I've held that unintentional feedback close to me ever since. Because we can win every trophy, title, newspaper headline there is, but if there are players that don't feel valued, a part of the success, or cared about by the coach, then we aren't winning at all.

In our quest for streaks, wins, and awards, we can certainly come out on top and be admired as the winningest coach around. **But there is no correlation to our team's record and our success as a coach.** That's the wrong unit of measure for what we are doing out there. I'm not saying that all the players have to like me, all the parents have to like me, and everything is perfect. Im saying that the definition of coach has never been a person who creates wins. I've coached all over the country and I've never been asked my win-loss record. I've never been hired or fired for it. I don't coach professional sports.

The definition of coach is someone who affects another positively – performance, mindset, belief, ability, motivation, resilience. **A coach makes a person better**. At no level does someone seek a coach to become miserable. Uncomfortable? YES! But if a coach takes away things like confidence, belief, vision, and the ability to perform to potential then we don't have a coach. We don't even have a leader. What we have, is a person with an ego problem and vision that includes the success of themselves by exploiting the ability of their player/client/etc.

At the time, when I was the "life ruiner" I wanted both. I wanted wins for myself. I wanted to prove that I was a good coach, and knew what I was doing. But I also wanted the players to be successful and share in those wins. I figured those two goals would feed into each other. Ego is a powerful beast, however. When we try to have both, ego mixes with emotions in the moment and it always wins. When ego is involved, the clash of best interests means someone has to lose. The ego can't survive without the win, so it will always fight to come out on top.

It was when I put myself out of the equation, fully committed myself to being a service driven leader who was there for the benefit of my players, that I was able to toss ego aside and strive to become a life **enricher**. Ironically, when we become that servant leader, a life enricher, who seeks the greatness in others and puts ourselves aside – we become successful as a biproduct. But the only way to learn that, was to let go, get humble, and find my greater purpose.

Love it or Leave it.

I'm turning 40 this fall, and as I've talked to my friends all reaching this "City Slickers" mid-life crisis age, I came to realize there is a theme to the chatter. Despite the blessings so many of us are surrounded by and truly appreciate, there are universal questions being asked. Am I doing what I'm supposed to be doing? Is this really the path I'm supposed to be on? Why don't I feel inspired, fulfilled, or excited to get out of bed in the morning? What happened to those big dreams we all talked about after high school, did I settle? Is the fun over?

Ironically, it's the same questions I hear from my athletes, and my fellow coaches out there. Am I doing this right? Why don't I feel more fulfilled and less beat down? What happened to that vision I had of success and winning and high fives? I know this is important, why am I struggling so much? These are questions that we all face when we reach a crossroads, get settled without growth, or become pressed to change but feel stuck and unable to do so. It's the questions we ask because we feel we are tied to our circumstance, rather than empowered to write the life we choose.

My mid-life crisis came a few years early, in my mid-thirties. It was more of a possible life-ending crisis that woke me up. I didn't want to left life happen to me anymore. I wanted to start building something. I began to re-write and re-wire my thinking, behavior, and learn to create my perceptions and daily decisions. I didn't have time to be in a rut, I didn't know if I had any time at all. Of course, the truth is none of us know if we have time and how much.

I've found three areas in my daily life that can drastically affect my state of mind, my state of productivity, my level of happiness, my perspective, and ability to share my talents and accomplish new things. When disconnects form in any of these areas, I feel myself sliding into that rut. **Only reconnecting with all three** has successfully pulled me back out.

1. Daily renewal of Faith, what I believe, my core, my center
2. Taking care of my body and my mind (exercise, food, reading/watching/mentoring/journaling info that makes me grow)

3. Sharing something that fills me with energy with someone else. Talking about something that makes me light up gets me back into that mindset daily

I can hobble along for a short while with one of those missing, maybe even two, but without fail – eventually my priorities, my feelings, ability to function will begin to deteriorate. Reconnecting all three has been the only path back. Ever start eating junk food for too long only to realize you don't feel like exercising anymore either? Low energy levels and sluggishness sets in, then the guilt. Motivation to grow your mind, or build your faith and core values drops down because you know you aren't treating yourself well. It's a cycle that's rarely broken without purposeful action.

After my embolism, I made a new path for myself based on this simple concept.

Love it, be passionate about it, have a purpose to it, and grow with it – OR DON'T DO IT.

I take this into everything I do now. That includes coaching; it includes what I expect from my athletes, my staff, my athlete's parents. It includes decisions about where to live, what jobs to accept, what commitments I make, where I spend my time.

Sometimes we have to take that place where we are right now, until we can make changes, and we have to grasp that ideal in any way that we can. All circumstances cannot be immediately changed, but our perception and our choices with what to do inside those can be changed in an instant. A difficult boss or co-worker, a nasty commute, low pay, too many hours, frustrations everywhere can be hard to overcome; especially if it's been going on to the point of breaking. For coaches it might be an AD, parent, player, hidden agendas, power struggles, or lack of support. Maybe you're not struggling but you're coasting, not growing, not excited anymore. Maybe it's just a rut.

Take that place where you are, uncomfortable or not, and incorporate time for activities that reconnect with your 3 points every day. Faith, Body/Mind, and Sharing Energy

Then make a list. Write down one thing that:
1. you love about it (or used to love about it)

2. makes you passionate about it (or could, or used too if you focused on it)
3. Gives you purpose when you do it well – why did you sign up for this in the first place? What's buried under the disappointment.
4. You can grow from this experience while you're in it

Now, write down a second list. How can you use a negative to work on each of the above goals?

For example: that commute time is causing major stress, download some inspiring personal growth audiobooks to listen to on the way home or record a voice memo journal, learn a new language, learn a skill that will help you at work, record messages for your kids or spouse to listen too at the end of the month or write that book you've always wanted to write by speaking it and recording it.

Example: Difficult parent and power struggle – nothing will help you grow like learning to mend relationships, build a support team, and find common goals. Every difficult parent I've encountered has taught me more about how people interact and how to be more compassionate, understanding, patient, firm in my beliefs and balancing my philosophy with conflict.

This is an exercise your athletes can do with you. Many of our kids are lacking coping skills for things that are difficult and because of that, many of them shut down when they feel things aren't going their way or making them happy. Give them back the driver seat. Help them build the tools they need to find their passion, excitement, and purpose.

Build your team an athlete workbook to help your players reframe their mindset, be empowered to rebuild their mental framework, write their own story, find the purpose and the passion behind the competition, grind, practice, sweat, and relationships. So many of our athletes are lacking coping skills, grit, and vision. As coaches', we have the ability to help them learn how to do this for themselves.

It's not just about being ALL IN, forcing a commitment because you said you would. Don't just be committed to something. The world is full of people who are simply committed to things for the sake of keeping a commitment, but with no passion or purpose in their task who are miserable – Find a way to Love it or Leave it

Positive Leadership

(leading to build and not break,
remembering why it matters)

Confessions of an Imperfect Coach

Dear Coach...

70 percent of kids drop out of sports by the age 13...[1]

Dear Coach,

I'm 11. I love lacrosse. My mom bought me my first stick this year for my birthday, it's blue – my favorite color. My dad restrung it for me from videos on YouTube. It's perfect.

I spend tons of time in the backyard running around with my stick, trying to hit trees with the ball and chasing my dog around while he tries to steal the ball from me.

I couldn't sign up for your travel team last summer because my family had too much going on and we didn't have enough money, but I thought those uniforms you picked out were amazing. I can't lie, I really wanted one and I wanted to be on that team. You seem to like the kids from your summer team a lot more than some of the other players. I'm going to ask my parents to get me signed up next summer!

Dear Coach,

I don't always know how you feel I'm doing at practice. I'm scared I'm going to make a mistake and get called out in front of the team. It's so embarrassing. That one time you high-fived me for doing something right – I'll never forget it! I replay that moment over and over. I haven't been able to get that again so I must not be doing anything right.

I try to do things that will catch your attention at practice but often when I do something right you're looking the other way and you miss it. Then I mess up right in front of you and you see it. I feel like I'm never going to get any better. You seem like you're in a hurry or busy, I'm scared to ask questions.

Dear Coach,

I sit on the bench a lot. Actually, I sit on the sideline a lot at practice too. It feels like I'm not important to the rest of the team. The first line stays in at practice forever. I love lacrosse

---

[1] *Physical Activity Counsel,*
http://www.physicalactivitycouncil.com/pdfs/current.pdf

but I'm so bored at practice that I know I'm getting distracted and not learning like I should.

I wish you would tell me I was doing something well. I wish you didn't yell at the whole team when one or two people are goofing around and I was trying so hard to show you that I care and want to be there. Do you see that I was standing quietly and listening and that I ran super-fast and collected the most ground balls after practice? My mom was mad at me for taking so long to leave practice but I knew you needed help. Did you notice?

Dear Coach,

You always seem mad at us unless we are winning or scoring. Do you care about us at all or are we just a record? When we win, you get so excited and pat us all on the back, but some of those teams are hard, sometimes we struggle, but we still felt like we tried really hard but you call us lazy if we don't win.

My mom's been sick in the hospital. Today you yelled at me when I misheard the directions and went the wrong way. Boys are supposed to be able to handle being yelled at. Why does it bother me so much? Getting yelled at during every practice is so hard after being in school all day. I thought lacrosse would be different than this. I'm no good and I'm having a hard time at home and at school.

Dear Coach,

I've decided I don't want to play anymore. I still love lacrosse but I don't really like being on a team. It seems like the players are always arguing and the coaches are always mad at us. Yesterday we ran for half an hour because we didn't win last night. I never even got a chance to play. In fact, I never do, but I always pay the team punishment. I wish I got the chance to help the team play better, I'm just not good enough.

Dear Coach,

Today is my 13th birthday, I gave my blue stick to a friend of mine who is thinking of playing. I don't need it anymore. I'm done with sports, what a waste of time.

Start Where You Are

The pressure to be like "Maryland", a state where lacrosse almost seems to be built into every kids DNA, is driving kids away from lacrosse in many developing areas. I grew up playing in Maryland, so I'm familiar with the difference between my home state and the developing lacrosse states I've lived in more recently as an adult, as a parent, and a coach.

My boys started playing lacrosse around age 9 in a developing area. That's also the year they stopped playing lacrosse. I signed them up for a Winter interest program that was held for them at an indoor gym in attempt to get kids to sign up for the Spring program. It was the first year they were old enough to participate and I had waited for this day to come! My boys were so excited! (ok I was also embarrassingly excited!) We bought and borrowed them gear and sticks and padded them up and sent them in to learn the sport that I have devoted my life to teaching and growing. I was more than a lax parent that night, I was a lax enthusiast in heaven!

Unable to control my curiosity, I peeked into the gym, excited to see them having fun. But what I saw instead was a high school like practice with drills, over coaching, long lines and local high school player *helpers* playing at 100% over top of these little guys instead of helping them. One of my boys was standing over on the side looking lost. My heart sank.

Being the direct person that I am, I asked one of the people leading the event if they considered making it a little more fun-centered since the goal is to attract these kids (9 year olds!) to the sport. The response I got was one that I would hear echoed in almost every new developing area I have been. The belief is that: *these kids are so behind the mid-Atlantic states, we can't afford to have them just play, we must catch them up so they can compete, so we can get as good as the kids in Maryland. They must start earlier, practice more, we don't have time for anything else. The kids who can't handle it will weed themselves out.*

Is this a youth sport or a professional lacrosse league training program? We are still talking about children, right?! My kids climbed into the car and I asked them how it was and they both said they were bored, it was too hard, and they didn't really want to go back. **And I watched the sport I loved die out of my house for 7 years until this year when both my boys, now in high school, are finally finding a love of lacrosse on the JV team together.**

I played in Maryland as a kid, high school athlete, and college athlete and I started learning by running around the yard, playing in silly lacrosse games with my older siblings in the backyard, and digging dirt with my dad's lacrosse stick. I fell in love with the game before I ever set foot inside any official team. I wasn't in an area that was lacrosse dominant because we started doing high school drills as kids; it was because we had the opportunity to play with fiddle stix in Ocean City, and gym glass lacrosse at school, had parents or relatives that let us lug around their giant stick and play with it, and we were exposed to the fun early on. It wasn't forced down our throats; we grew into it as part of our culture and lifestyle and we considered it play. Then when we found our teams to play on, the love of the sport was already there and the drive to improve came naturally on an already solidly built foundation.

Whatever area you are in, no matter what age the kids are who come out to play for the first time, they must fall in love with it first. For some kids, they haven't even fallen in love with the idea of sports yet, let alone any specific one. US Lacrosse shared a video, by 'about the kids,' of little boys running around penguins and then trying to put the balls into the net and I realized, this program has got it right! The intensity and the high-level skills will come, no matter what age they start playing, but ONLY if they first learn to love the game and grow the desire to move on.

Our job for our new players (regardless of age) is to foster a love of the game, confidence, and the opportunity to participate in fun competition (rather than waiting in line or sitting on a bench) and then our job as coaches becomes easy. Kids who love it will come to us and ask for guidance. If we build the foundation, they will pull the sticks out on their own and go play on their own time, show up for practice anxious for what's next, and develop on their own timeline – as they develop physically, emotionally, and mentally – but to their full potential. If I find myself struggling to get kids to work on their skills, the first thing I look at is my practice plan – am I making this sport fun or a chore? No one wants to go home and practice chores!

Our drive to compete with the mid-Atlantic states is back firing on our kids as we try to rush them into skills that must naturally take place at a pace that is right for them. It's not a race to outdo a state that's had lacrosse for as long as I can remember, but a journey to grow quality options that start right where we are. The patient teaching and reinforcing of fundamentals and the fun will drive the development faster than any other method.

Recently I was observing a practice and I overheard a coach yelling to a small kid to hold onto his stick, that it isn't a toy. Immediately I felt defiant for this kid. It most certainly IS a toy! PLAY ON!

Coach Vs. School Teacher

As I walked around the track on my son's practice field – trying to squeeze in some extra steps for the day, headphones in, audible book playing (the Seed by Jon Gordon), I did what I usually do when I'm out around playing fields; I people watch. My son's team and the other high school team were practicing, I snuck in a few peeks as he made some great stops in the goal and I (admittedly) cringed a few times when he forgot to step to the ball. Even over the sound of my audiobook, I could hear the team cheering Drew on to the goal – "Great Job Drew," "Nice Stop Drew!" "Drew's a Wall!" Drew got in the car at the end of practice feeling great about playing lacrosse. (I love those days!)

Unfortunately, I'm afraid that some kids had a less positive ride home experience. On the baseball fields to my right as I rounded the bottom of the lacrosse field, I could see the body language and actually (through my headphones and from at least a full football field away), could HEAR the baseball coach who was working with what appeared to be late elementary or early middle school aged kids. I heard the words 'worthless,' 'stupid,' and 'deaf' ring out, and then the F bomb. Immediately I looked at the other parent helpers on the field waiting for them to step in angrily, but they were nodding. NODDING.

I kept walking trying to tune out the outside and focus on listening to my book. As I rounded the other side of the field, I saw the most adorable little bobble head and his dad working on some post practice skills. So cute, I couldn't help but smile! Bobble heads are the kids whose helmets are bigger than their shoulders, young kindergarten to 2nd grade age range. It's one of my favorite age groups to watch because everything they do is adorable and fantastic as they wield equipment and sticks much bigger and heavier than they are. But as the path brought me closer I realized this wasn't father and son fun. This was frustrated parent and a little boy with his head hanging low. "Why can't you FOLLOW INSTRUCTIONS?" "It's SO EASY!" The boy dropped the next pass, the small possibly 5 or 6-year old whose helmet was almost bigger than his entire body, dropped the pass. He connected with it, but it bounced out. For me, that's a high five moment! His dad chucked his stick down on the ground. Then picked up the ball and chucked that too. "Why can't you do it?! You aren't going home until you start listening!"

I kept walking, feeling for that kid, wanting some patient lax person to show up and offer to step in. Wanting to remind that dad that these days don't last and neither do the opportunities to grow a trusting teaching relationship. But I kept going.

Running around in the grass outside the field were kids leaving football training. Tiny little first grade guys who had just trained agility and speed like the big boys do, parents talking about future scholarships and scouts. On top of that I could still hear the baseball coach, it had been 10 minutes and the kids were still being yelled at, they had barely moved an inch. At this point the chatter from the fields around me forced me to turn up my headphones, I couldn't bear to hear anymore. I wanted to call over all the kids and tell them that they were about to go to *Kate's Fun Sports Camp* where parents can't come unless they promised to just encourage and coaches had to be kind and patient – but then I remembered I didn't have my ruby slippers and how on earth could I pull that one off?

Coaches are teachers, it's what we do. We may not be in a classroom, but there is no question that our job is to teach kids a skill, a game, rules, how to behave, how to work with others, how to be respectful, and how to be ready for the next level. In fact, the two ideals are so alike that if you aren't teaching, is it fair to say you aren't really coaching?

So, if coaches are teachers, shouldn't we use teaching principles and tactics so that our kids can learn? Can you imagine standing in front of a classroom throwing a tantrum because a kid didn't understand a math problem, maybe tossing a pen violently at the floor, stomping your foot, and throwing your hat? How about dropping a few curse words and forcing them to run because they still can't spell that difficult word or because they forgot their homework? Know any effective teachers with highly motivated students that tell their students to their face that they are lazy, or that even first graders can do it?

For some reason, this bully behavior has become acceptable, normal, and dare I say even a mark of a strong coach of our children. It's considered a style or philosophy. I'd like to call it something else, ineffective and occasionally abusive.

Confessions of an Imperfect Coach

What do we know about great teachers that we can absolutely take to the field?

Great Coaches...

1. **Are fun** – they make whatever subject they are teaching fun, hands on, and applicable to the kids' lives who are learning it.
2. **Are patient** – they understand that it takes many tries, sometimes explaining it in different ways, and they also help keep the kids from getting frustrated so they don't quit trying.
3. **Praise effort** – they notice when hard work is happening, and it creates an atmosphere where kids work hard to get noticed.
4. **Hold kids accountable** – they communicate the rules and consequences clearly and they calmly and in control, enforce them.
5. **Mix things up** – they keep the kids interested by doing new things, keeping the kids on their toes.
6. **Use kind words** – they make a safe environment where kids feel free to try things and explore and push their limits by speaking in a way that is respectful and kind.
7. **Stay even tempered even when pushed** – they create a stable and reliable atmosphere where emotions don't bounce all over the place.
8. **Give feedback** – kids are told daily/weekly/monthly how they are doing, where they are falling short, and where they are excelling through grades and comments. They are approached when they seem to be not progressing and offered help to improve.
9. **Give kids choices** – they offer some sense of buy-in and control over daily options by finding ways to let kids choose even a small part of the learning activity when possible.
10. **Encourage questions and free thinking** – they allow kids to ask why, to encourage them to try it and see why, to learn by doing in a controlled environment and to self-advocate when they don't understand.

It's our job as coaches, whether we are training a league, camp, clinic, team, or even our own kid to remember that there's a method to teaching and there's a strategy for effective learning. Our emotions and fight or flight in the moment can lead us down a path we should not take with kids just because it's a sport and not Math or English. Kids may react immediately to bullying by doing what you want, but in the long term we're going to lose these athletes who eventually learn they don't have to take it anymore. If we want to keep kids in sports then we must foster a love of learning and teach them in a way where they find success in the short term and the long term —and that comes through being an effective teaching-focused coach when we step onto that field.

Open Heart, Open Mind

I feel confident in my ability to read people. This served me very well when I was in sales, and has been helpful in all my leadership roles and relationships in general. I remember the first time I learned about how I seem to absorb and detect the emotions around me without even realizing it.

I was watching a movie and I heard whispering around me. I looked around and found all eyes in the room on me with amused expressions. "WHAT?! What are you looking at?" I cried out defensively...

Apparently, the news circulating the room was that every emotion the characters in the movie were feeling, I was acting out with my facial expressions, completely unaware I was doing it. If someone was sad; my face would crumple. If they were happy; I would be smiling. If they were tense; my worry lines would pop up.

If we are being honest here, I also absorb accents, which is much worse. If I speak to someone with any sort of accent, it is only a matter of a few sentences before I suddenly have one too, and it's not a very good imitation. I've heard myself doing it and I try to stop, but at this point I think it's just a part of me that I can't help! So, if I've done it to you, I'm sorry! (please read that sentence back in whatever accent you may have so that it's authentic).

But even with people reading skills, I was no match for my players' ability to hide what they were feeling or thinking because they didn't feel comfortable bringing difficult conversations to me. I hold the key to playing time, rewards, consequences, and that makes me unapproachable to a certain extent no matter how nice I may be on that field. I needed a way to get feedback that would help me gauge where the team was inside their heads in an honest and open way.

Eventually I wanted to get to the point where we could gather as a team and openly discuss our feelings about the season, but we couldn't just start there. That kind of openness needs practice, and trust built first, and I couldn't build the trust without the openness.

I felt stuck.

So, I came up with a mid-season player questionnaire that was anonymous and it had a dual purpose. First, it gave the team a chance to tell me what they are really thinking and air out some things they may have been holding inside or struggling with that need my attention. Second, it made them sit down and think about some important questions about being a teammate, their own effort level, and where we could go from this point on.

I was surprised at the feedback, at the undercurrents I was unaware even existed. I was also in awe of the deeply caring and thoughtful responses I got back. The team had much more going on than what is shown on the surface. I found this exercise incredibly eye opening and even bonding experience to allow ourselves to see all the layers in our programs and tend to the hearts and needs of each contributor.

Going over some of the common answers with the team allowed for the conversation to deepen, and for issues to be brought out more easily in the future because the comfort level, and trust, hopefully would be there.

Here is the questionnaire I provided to the team:

Questions for the team to answer and return, typed and anonymous:

1. **SKILLS:** What do you believe your skill strengths are on this team? Where do you think you would like to see improvement in yourself? What skills do you feel the team needs to work on more? What skills do you feel are not improving the way they should? What skills are a strength for our team? Where do you feel the effort level is during drills and conditioning? Do you feel pushed in your performance or could you give more?

2. **TEAMMATE:** What do you feel you bring to the team as a teammate? Where would you like to see improvement in your teammate abilities? Where would you like to see improvement in your teammates' team unity abilities? Do you feel the team is encouraging, respectful, and working together? If not, what do you perceive to be issues that need to be addressed?

3. **LEARNING NEW SKILLS AND TACTICS:** How effectively do you feel the practice formats are in helping your particular learning style? Is there anything that would assist you in learning?
4. **DRILLING:** How effectively do you feel the practice formats are in assisting you to perform tasks with your teammates and improve team play? Is there anything you believe would improve this process?
5. **COACHING:** Do you feel the coach is approachable when you need clarification on sport related topics? Do you feel the coach is approachable when you need guidance outside of skills? Do you feel your concerns are taken seriously and you have the opportunity to contribute your own ideas to the team? Do you find corrections to be clear, concise, and respectful? Is there something you would like to see improved in the way the coach communicates with you at practice, during games, or other?

It takes a very service oriented mindset to open yourself to criticism as a coach, especially in today's climate where we already face a pile of critiques and complaints every day. But this is different, it's a culture growing and constructive way for us to bond with our players, meet their needs, and reconnect with them.

When we stop growing as leaders we are no longer effective, relevant, or of any use to our team – let the team help you grow the way we love helping our teams grow.

Build Not Break

Imagine being 10 years old, you just ran up and down a field for close to an hour with only a few breaks. You're in front of a small crowd of cheering and jeering parents, a few expectant coaches and intimidating referees with whistles giving constant directions and penalties. You've only held a stick in your hand a few weeks and the game is a little confusing. There are phrases you are still learning, lines all over the field with different meanings, rules galore, new movements you haven't heard before like cutting, spacing, mirroring, and athletic stance. There are fine motor skills that are sometimes a bit out of your reach and now pressure to do those skills with another team chasing after you and all those people watching. The other team keeps scoring, the coach is getting louder, and you can hear your dad shouting to "get the ground balls!" and another parent yelling that the team needs to "wake up." You're thinking that you're anything but asleep, running your heart out and trying to process a ton of new info. You feel overwhelmed, excited, and yet still having a good time out there with your friends who occasionally pass by and share a giggle.

The game ends and you're feeling the pressure of being defeated by a 10-goal differential, you're feeling like maybe you'll never get this game, thinking about your mistakes and trying to do that thing that kids do when they goof around and cover their vulnerability with jokes and redirecting attention away from the coaches that could be upset with them, that they fear they may have let down. The coach calls everyone in and you're looking to your teacher, your leader and ready to hear what wisdom he or she is ready to pass onto an already slowly fading attention span.

Now imagine that your coach tells your team that you aren't in very good condition, you were breathing too heavy, and moving too slow. You aren't working hard enough outside of practice on your stick skills and you didn't focus enough at the last practice. You aren't listening to directions because you didn't execute the skills on the field. You looked lost, you won't get better if you don't work harder. All the blame is placed on the players, and the game is all about where you went wrong.

Now you know why so many kids drop out of sports.

Confessions of an Imperfect Coach

I heard 4 coaches post-game talks that day as I hung around the rec field with my daughter after her game and each one was a painful reminder that we have so far to go in understanding what positive coaching is all about. These well-meaning coaches were seeking a performance boost by calling out shortcomings, but instead gave the team a serious confidence problem.

Self-confidence is one of the biggest obstacles kids face that hold them back from playing at their best. Kids who are empowered don't just keep playing sports, they also perform significantly higher and gain more skills. As adults, we've forgotten how intimidating the set-up of games is and just how much information we are throwing at them in short, sometimes cold, and late-night practices. Hesitation to get the ball, or make a cut, or drive to play defense isn't sleepiness; it's fear, it's uncertainty. To eliminate those obstacles we, as coaches and parents, must supply and nurture a culture that Builds instead of Breaks.

I coach mostly females these days, and I can say in all certainly that the worst thing you can do to a girl who already innately negative self-talks herself in miserable circles, is give her a list of failures, especially effort based ones like not working hard enough or hustling. Reinforcing these sources of low self-esteem is asking for performance to decrease, the very opposite of the effect you are likely hoping for.

End your games instead with celebrations, even if you lose, even if the team looked like one big hot mess from warm up to the final whistle, even if half the team was late and the other half was giggling non-stop. These aren't college athletes, they're kids, that are in fact -there to have fun. They signed up because they want to be there, they want to play, learn, and be somewhere with their friends other than school where they are always being told to stop talking and being silly. Direct the fun by offering fun activities during warm up time and at practice, celebrate the silliness with them – it keeps us young, and then ask them to respect the times when you are teaching – but keep those times very short and very concise and fill the other spaces with praise and celebrations.

Where did they try hard? Who gets an effort point? Who did something that maybe didn't work out but was brave to try it? How did they make you proud today? Why do you love coaching your team – remind them at every game and every practice why you show up again and again-because of them, because you care about THEM, because you believe in THEM. Admit coaching fails; we fail at every game, become human with them, you all learned from mistakes together. Ask them to call out what they thought others did well, what did the other team do well that they can try to emulate. Ask them what they feel like they need help with at the next practice and you may be surprised just how much they understand but are just struggling to execute because they need more experience at doing it.

Leave the corrections for the next practice, not the post-game talk. Let them leave that game still loving it, and believing that they are growing as players even if they haven't gotten it all figured out just yet. Your words as a coach can change a kid's outlook on not only sports, but on how they feel about themselves and their abilities. That's a lot of power and responsibility, and though we will always continue our journey to get better and win games, we can't ever let that pursuit of winning overshadow the reason we are out there in the first place.

Two Paths Diverged in Coaching

*"... if you are a coach or manager building a team,
remember that whatever you try to build with fear will
eventually crumble. But that which is built with love will endure.
If you build your team with love they will become more and do
more than you ever thought possible.
Most of all, as you build with love, know that you will face
many challenges and negative forces that can shift your focus
back to fear if you let it. When this happens decide to LOVE ALL
OF IT. When you love all of it you will fear none of it." Jon
Gordon*

Ironically, at the end of both journeys, I ended up in similar placings with our record, stats, and success. That's an important fact in this, so take note. But here's where we ended in very different places; it was in our team culture over all, our amount of injuries, and the amount of friction between coach/player/parent, our joy, and our stress.

It was at the end of these two journeys that I forever changed as a coach, and ironically as a parent, and a person. Not only did Journey 1 teach me that I was not doing it right, but Journey 2 taught me that it's not about me at all, it's about fostering a love of the process and letting go of the fears of an outcome that might make us look like we don't know what we're doing.

Journey 1:
- High expectations/very little flexibility.
- Required player commitment/personally feeling disrespected when they chose something they thought was more important with their time. Spring break was a thorn in my side – how could they leave for a week?!
- Longer and more practices, no or rare days off, rarely done on time, never satisfied at the end, long tedious drills with lots of teaching. Lectures at the end about doing better tomorrow.

- Direct call outs to players not meeting the standard. Pressure to perform or be used as the example of what not to do so we could get fixed as a team faster.
- Fun time was earned, it could be taken away if effort/performance wasn't to satisfaction.
- Everything was a drill. Everything had to have order.
- Fun was built in as an option, if earned during the season, but I was disconnected from it. By the time they got anything fun planned, it was because things had gotten so miserable I was grasping at straws to bring them back in.
- Relied on communicating with players who I felt were happy, avoided those I felt were not because maybe it felt safer? I was frustrated? I'm not sure, but it was easier (until it got bigger than me).
- I strictly held a 'don't talk to me about playing time & don't question my methods' policy. I basically built a wall. 'I'm the coach. You're not.'
- Great success on the field. Great success in stats. Great overall record! Woohoo it's working! (eye roll)
- Felt increasingly empty and frustrated as a coach. Felt like I was dragging my players through the season. Felt like I cared about getting to our goals more than them. Could see their enthusiasm dropping one by one as time went on. Why were they so much less excited about playing the second half of the season??? (duh!)
- Put most of my effort into the hard-core athletes, their parents were the most supportive of my all-out methods.
- Watched the number of uncoachable players grow every week. Couldn't figure out why. Blamed their commitment.
- I pointed out often where players were falling short. Out of shape, bad stick work, no commitment. I was always focused on where we weren't doing well. I stopped seeing improvements because I just kept seeing more flaws.

Journey 2:

Confessions of an Imperfect Coach

- High expectations/reasonable flexibility (school, family related, other sport related activities).
- Required Player commitment/but also had understanding that they have other commitments, balancing my coaching to prepare for those missing players as long as it wasn't a playoff, helping them understand when something was not a 'good enough reason' to miss because of the effects on the team as a whole and when it was ok. Good life lessons on understanding priorities.
- Spring Break: I started going on spring break myself. Best decision I ever made. Came back a day or two early and had a light stick work practice with those who were around and made it fun (did beach theme one year). I sent them off on spring break with a fun practice (speed gun and a piñata in the goal, relay races with fake mustaches on, dodge ball, and a scrimmage with water balloon balls). Remind them they want to come back because they love playing together. We started a contest for those who checked in the most on a group message with a picture or video of their workouts. (Yes, with all this fun, we STILL finished in the same place, if not BETTER than the season where it was nothing but hours and hours of drilling. Because the effort level and hearts were in the practices and they were fresh and fearless at games. Best lesson I ever learned!)
- Chose my battles to be inflexible on. Attitude and kindness to fellow players, drug and alcohol policy, grades.
- I let go. This is huge. If I tied my worth to my team's success, I guaranteed myself misery and sentenced my players to the same fate. Too many coaches have tied themselves to their team's performance and behavior. They shine back a reflection of your coaching, but they are not YOU. Our worth as coaches, ironically, has a lot more to do with how we treat our players than our records.
- I limited practice, not only on a daily basis, but overall. I cut down from 6 to 5 practices, didn't go more than 2 hours unless for a special prep, involved film watching,

etc. I always gave my players advanced notice and asked their permission to go longer. **I do not own their time just because we are in season.** I sent them home when they showed signs of over load from learning hard concepts, especially if they had been working hard. I inserted team building and fun into the week with no strings attached. They didn't lose it if they didn't perform, they earned it by making it on the team. It's a part of what we do.

- I used Show, Do, and Tell for everything, and allowed several days of different approaches for a concept to stick before I even consider getting frustrated. Short bursts of learning, and then moved on. I walked into each new drill with zero expectation of anything other than exposing the players to the concept. On average, it takes 3 times for things to click. Too often, we go from intro to game and don't understand why the transition isn't there.

- I let them teach. I used to talk too much. I knew I could say it better, so why not hear it from me? They learned faster this way. Teach each other, figure things out. I let them try it a couple different ways and then tell me which one worked and which one didn't and why.

- I stopped telling them they were doing it wrong. I started telling them where it was right, and where to look for making it better.

- I put myself in their shoes before I spoke. Figuratively of course, but I started thinking about what would I need said to me at that moment if I was them, instead of what could I say that would make ME feel better right now.

- I started an open-door policy where parents and players could ask me anything or check in, as long as it was about their own child or themselves.

- I had the same success ironically with this laid-back approach. Some might say, those teams had even more success. I enjoyed coaching 99.9% of the time. My players loved their season, start to finish. Highest numbers of parent support ever.

Two journeys, each finding success, one building wins in any way that works, and the other markedly building something incredible, memorable, and enjoyable.

The only way to take Journey 2, is to surrender the outcome. Let Go. focus on the players, their development as players and as people, see what they need in the big picture of life rather than just what they can do to bring in the W. Let go of your fear of losing, or falling short, and love the process. Because ultimately, the process built with heart, will take you where you want to go.

Small Decisions, Big Impact. Word Choice.

We make a lot of small decisions on a daily basis that have various amounts of impact in our coaching. Over the course of a year, the amount of small decisions we make can feel overwhelming. Some we make with more thought than others, some with haste, some after much procrastination, some we delegate to someone else to handle, and some with emotion.

Some of those decisions make little impact on our players and our program, some may seem small but cause all sorts of conspiracy theories about your intentions to surface. We can get caught up in small decisions, trying not to rock the boat, we can lose ourselves in the pile of small decisions surrounding us.

This is the reason why knowing our purpose, our beliefs, and having a clearly defined vision is vital to coaches. This is what keeps us on the right track no matter the chaos surrounding us.

- Does this decision bring me closer to my team's vision?
- Is it in line with my purpose as a coach, educator, and leader?
- Will my players' perception of this decision be in line with my known philosophy?

One of the decisions we make every single day is **how we decide to talk to our players** (including in person, through messaging, email, etc.). We're short on time, sometimes emotionally charged up, we want to fix this yesterday, and we see potential and want to charge full speed ahead. After all, they can take it. They're athletes, right?

But will it derail our progress, our culture, and our belief system if we disregard how our message comes across? Can we finally break the old-fashioned belief that trying to make the message about believing they can do better rather than shaming them for doing poorly is weak or coddling? It's been proven repeatedly that teams who are secure in their core that their coaches believe in their abilities, even when they fail, perform BETTER in the long run than coaches who use fear and shaming as a tactic for short term results. Let's embrace that edge and use it! But it's not just game day, or team talks that matter. It's every single interaction, even those small ones that we don't put much thought into. Sometimes, it's even our lack of words that can break someone. Are they searching for some sort of explanation or feedback that isn't coming?

Example of word choice for the same goal:

Option 1: "There's going to be a lot more running, you guys are slow and out of shape, that was embarrassing." True? Probably. Quick? Yes! Did you just tell them they are slow and an embarrassment? Yup. Hard to convince them at the next game that they can be better? Maybe. Are they excited for change or dreading the next round of hill sprints and possible insults?

Option 2: "How did you guys feel at the last game with your speed and conditioning? Did anyone feel like they were struggling out there? I definitely feel like we have the athleticism on this team to improve on that and really outrun them instead. How much time do you think we should add on at practice to catch ourselves up? Anyone want to lead conditioning outside practice on the weekends? Let's do a time test today and then retest and see how we do, how does two weeks sound? Team goal for time improvement?"

What's the difference in the two messages? If you take out the subject of conditioning and speed, what message did they hear about themselves as a team and individually as players from their coach?

The words you choose may be the most important decision you make in these kids' lives. Each sentence or phrase may be a small decision made repeatedly day in and day out. But the sum of those words can build or break your players, your team, your culture, and your program. Your goal of improving skills is the same, but how you choose to motivate them can bring about drastically different results in the performance, self-esteem and overall experience. Choose them carefully.

RESET! Squash the Drama

It's about half-way through the season. It started off strong, with players excited, parents cheering, and practices new and interesting. But somewhere around the halfway point something starts shifting. Cliques are beginning to form. Playing time is questioned (even if it's pretty equal). Frustration may be bubbling under the surface. And then one day... you have the worst practice/game/tournament ever and it seems completely out of hand.

What happened? Some seasons have underlying drama that simply implodes before you, as a coach, even knew it was there. You felt something was off; their effort wasn't the same, their mental toughness wasn't there, and they're now suddenly missing passes, shots, slides that they used to get. Here's the equally important part many of us miss – we're not nearly as positive as we were at the beginning of the season either. We are getting short with the refs and easily frustrated at players. Maybe dealing with a few parents. Playing some unsportsmanlike teams. Having games with half the team sick or injured and getting pummeled helplessly. A little exhausted from balancing full-time job, our own families, and practices followed by weekend tourneys. With all of that going on, it's bound to make a little of our light go out and we often don't even realize it. That negativity and strain transfers to our players and is reflected back at us, but rarely do we make that correlation.

You can let this continue and decide that the drama isn't part of your job, but it can spiral quickly. You can simply tell them to shape up. You can run them until they can't focus on anything else. You can just blame it on your athletes being females (this response is my least favorite of all).

OR...

You can hit RESET and teach them a better way to be a great teammate and build their confidence as you do it.

If you're staring down the ugly eye of team culture gone wrong, here's how you can get it back and be stronger on the other side for it:

1. Remember that they are kids, still learning how to communicate. They are still learning how to read body

Confessions of an Imperfect Coach

language, understand sarcasm, and they are incredibly insecure no matter how confident they may appear. They are reacting to how they feel, they aren't trying to sabotage the team even if they are successfully doing it.

2. Be aware that their parents likely have no idea they are a mess at practice, stirring the pot with their teammates, throwing an attitude because that may not be the side they are showing at home and they are in a different setting there.

3. Have a parent meeting, brief and to the point. We are struggling with negativity. It's negative self-talk, its lack of confidence, and it's negative talk between teammates and behind each other's backs. Our goal is to work on reinforcing positive behavior, call out high levels of effort and trying new things with praise, and stopping the negative self-talk in its tracks. I've never had this meeting and had parents not look completely surprised, they often just didn't know and the turn around when parents buy in is incredible. Remember, parents truly do want the same things we do as coaches – happy, growing, developing kids with character who are getting better at their sport.

4. Have a team meeting. Don't hold back and sugar coat it; be straight forward but kind. Boundaries make kids feel safer. You will many times be surprised at the positive reaction that kind and caring boundaries will create. "You are here to play ___insert sport___. When you come to practice, you are here to get better at this sport. If you don't want to be at practice, don't take away from the players that want to learn. You have the choice to stay home or chose another activity. If you want to come, we will be training you to get better. Sometimes it will be fun, sometimes it will be hard, sometimes it won't be your favorite thing. This opportunity is for those who want it. These are your teammates, your job is to work with them, support them, and help them grow, as well as to offer your very best to them. There will be no negativity tolerated towards another teammate or towards yourself.

5. Talk about where the team is going. We have this many games left, this many weeks of practice, fun events,

tournaments, dinners, and tons of fun. We want every single player here to experience all of this. But only the players who agree to be all-in will be continuing on this journey with us.

6. Hand out team pledges (below is one of mine I used for a middle school travel team). Give them a week to look it over with their parents, sign it, and hand it in. Express how valuable each player is and that you want every single player on board making life-long friends and building memories, but that they need to be sure when they sign it that they are committed to the pledge.

7. Leave it at that. Tell them how much you enjoy coaching them, that you care about them and their experience, and then end the meeting. It is incredibly important that your delivery is firm, but also driven by love. They can feel if you are doing this for their best interest. Don't go into this meeting with any anger in your heart.

8. Let the reset happen. Show up at the next practice with a high energy fun drill and a lot of high fives. Bring contagious positivity to propel you forward and encourage players as they make efforts towards encouraging other players. Give real praise – praise an effort or attempt of a new skill with no correction, no strings attached. We tend to sandwich everything with the intention of being positive but it's over instruction; sometimes they just need the high five.

9.

SAMPLE TEAM PLEDGE:

My Pledge to the team:

Believe in the abilities and efforts of my fellow teammates.

Encourage and build up my teammates.

Play hard and put out my best effort at practices and in games.

Think of what the team's needs are FIRST before my own.

Not allow negativity to get inside our team atmosphere, and I will not contribute to negativity.

Focus on being the best I can be in whatever role I am playing inside of our team.

Focus on solutions instead of problems.

Value all teammates and treat them with kindness and respect, both in their presence and when I am not with them.

I will talk positively about myself and continue to improve on where I feel I have weaknesses without quitting.

Seek help from coaches and support from teammates when I am frustrated.

If you're all in, sign the bottom and return to coach at practice this week.

Your WIFI is down Coach. Stop Yelling at it.

Here's the bottom line coaches. We have information that we need our players to know. We have new info, corrections, instructions, and questions that need to be answered. Our players need to hear and absorb this info, the quicker the better. They need to think about it, understand it, and manipulate it in their minds so they can go and apply it.

For this transaction to take place successfully we need WIFI. By that I mean, we need a connection to send this info through. Connections require two sides that are effectively working – the sending side needs to send out a clear message that alerts the receiver that it applies to them, is safe to hear, and grabs their interest. The receiving side needs to be in the correct state of mind to process that info, feel that it applies to them, is more interesting than the surrounding distractions, and start the processing sequence or it all drops and we must start over.

Here's what I see going on all over the place with teams – Our WIFI is down. It's broken. The connection isn't there so we do what every good person does when the WIFI is down, we get louder, irritated, frustrated, start blaming and pointing fingers and throwing our hands up in the air. Ever see a half time talk look like that?

If your players aren't eagerly awaiting information and excited to try it out, there's a good chance that your connection is down. Forcing the info at a louder, angrier, or more anxious tone won't make it get through any better. Adding some insults, doubts, and questioning their effort, commitment, or ability will quickly cut off a connection, sometimes permanently.

You must fix the connection if you want to fix the players. If you want anything to get through, this must happen first or you'll feel like your battling, dragging, pleading and banging your head to the end of your season.

Two coaches, side by side. One is yelling, pointing out mistakes, and failures to a group of players whose heads are dropping lower by the second. Maybe they aren't even paying attention, maybe they've shut off. The second coach is looking into the eyes of a team that is requesting to learn. The coach is explaining, answering questions, and looking for where things are working and going well to a group of players who are processing the info and figuring out how to apply it. Which one do you see yourself as? What reflects back at you when you talk to your team? If it's shame, fear, indifference, or boredom; then you're OFFLINE.

There is no benefit to yelling. None. You can scream at a broken connection all day but you'll never get the info through. Connect with your players and send them information that they will be receptive to. Info that will challenge them to think about how they can apply it. Send it in a way that helps them know you are giving them this info because you believe they can execute the ideals behind it. See the difference in a team connected with their coach, and feel the difference in your stress level and enjoyment of coaching.

How do you build connections?

- Value them equally as much when they fall as when they rise. Consistently.
- Hold them accountable, but don't live inside a box of rules and consequences.
- Talk to them with respect.
- Allow them to be human. Allow yourself to be human. Vulnerability and forgiveness are not weakness.
- Empathy. You can't be too hard on a player if you truly allow yourself to feel what they are feeling as you go into a conversation. You'll know better what they need and choose words wisely.
- Remember that you are in a position of people development. You are never the game-maker shifting chess pieces for a title, trophy, or a banner. Develop the players to their max potential, and let them fight for the win with the tools you provide.

How's your team's connection? Is your WIFI down or going strong?

What's in a Coach?

In an over-accessible but under-connected world, what value do we hold as coaches?

Before email, team group chats, apps, and instant messaging, we may have struggled to get our communications out but we haven't gotten any better at communicating now despite our abundance of accessible ways to contact each other.

Quantity and quality often have an inverse relationship. The easier it becomes to access each other instantly, the less thought, time, and care go into the actual communication. I find it ironic that the trend now for over the top prom invitations seems so romantic except that they almost always end with the person reading the invitation for themselves off a big piece of poster board instead of a meaningful face to face interaction.

This world is full of people who are accessible to one another, often instantly, and yet are craving that deeper relationship. We need more meaningful conversations, not faster ways to get a hold of each other.

What's in a coach? What can we provide to growing athletes who spend a large portion of their day accessing each other via texts and social media. To athletes who still feel alone and unable to connect on a deeper level, to work through the incredible stresses involved in adolescents and sorts?

We can connect instead of simply communicating. We don't have to merely inform, carry out the transaction of transferring knowledge and just another version of providing instant access. When we focus on just teaching skills we are becoming just another motivational quote, or "how to" video, like the ones they scroll through every day.

Try this and see if your players become more connected.

5 steps to connecting with your players:

1. Greet every player as they arrive at practice. Try asking them one specific question about something you know they have going on in their life. (How's that math class going, is the teacher still moving super-fast through the material? Did you find anyone to help you with that?)

2. Learn their names the first day. This is tough, especially if you work with several teams like I do. Get dollar store headbands and write their names on them, put tape on their helmet, repeat

Confessions of an Imperfect Coach

their name every time you talk to them and make sure you talk to each player at least 5 times that first practice.

3. Have check-ins. Let players pick a day everyday couple weeks to meet after practice and let you know what they've been up, how they are feeling, and if they need anything from you.

4. Notice things, pay attention. Are they acting different? A change of behavior or mood especially over time is a strong signal that you need to have that check in sooner rather than later. Sometimes it helps to have them just know that you have their back, whatever it is. Sometimes it's more than that, and they need real help and direction from someone like a school counselor.

5. Identify skills. Figure out what positive trait each player brings to the team and write them down. Spend the season reinforcing that value and expressing how much you appreciate it.

Are You A Label Maker?

How is it that some coaches come into a sport and create teams that surpass all their surrounding areas and become a dominating force? What do they know that other coaches don't? What's the secret to long lasting, quick forming, consistent success?

There's the obvious,

- that some coaches put in a lot of time into educating themselves and studying the game
- make meticulous plans for practice
- break down film and scout players
- getting their kids excited about playing in the off season.

But there's something else, something that makes an even bigger difference then all of that combined. And it's available for you to put into practice and reap the rewards as well!

It's about being a coach that sees players as multi-dimensional, and then getting to know those players and making connections so that every single athlete is being developed to their full potential. It's about keeping out the negativity that comes with labels, frustration, and giving up on each other.

Do you remember when those little electronic label makers came out? You type in a word and it prints out a little, perfect, clean label that sticks on anything. Those machines were fun, I got a little obsessed with labeling things. But there's a place where labels are anything but fun...

We tend to classify players. We don't have a lot of time to prep for a season and it's easiest to get to know a player to a certain extent and then put a label on them, throw them into a category, and leave them there until they prove to us otherwise. Problem is, our job is to lead them to that change, understand how they learn; not wait for them to figure it out and bring it to us.

Is that player with an attitude just going to drive you crazy all season? *Yea you know the one I'm talking about, the one you're hoping maybe doesn't come back next season.* These players are easy to write off, start assuming they're a bad egg, an energy vampire. But would it make sense to figure out what their deal is and work with them to find a better way to process, learn, and communicate? These are kids. Keep in mind that most of them have a direct cause behind their behavior. Some of my most difficult players have become team leaders and people I highly respect. Yes, that takes more time, but being great as a team and a coach often does.

Is your player hogging the ball? Do your teammates have trust built in each other? Are they able to recognize when it's safe to pass and when it's better to keep moving yourself? Are their supports and cutters getting into line of sight and inside an open passing lane? Is it fear of making a decision?

Is your player constantly late, never attending outside activities? Is there an issue with getting there, a responsibility at home holding them back perhaps? Are they feeling intimidated or like an outsider and uncomfortable at these activities? Do they not understand the purpose or buy in on team building?

Are they always goofing off at practice? Are they lost, having trouble learning with the teaching style you are using, constantly being distracted by another player, stressed by something else going on just before or after practice every day? Do they have trouble with organizing ideas, focusing, or need verbal cues when learning but they are afraid to ask and be a pain? Many kids are afraid to admit when they don't understand, so they'd rather just stay lost.

For every problem there is a solution, but you can't find it until truly getting to know your players. *The greatness and longevity of success comes from a coach caring about attacking the issues and understanding obstacles rather than looking at behavior and sticking that label over their heads.* Some of the most successful coaches I know can rattle off every detail about their players, know their favorite topics at school, their strengths, weaknesses, how they handle pressure, and how they learn best. It's inspiring to see that kind of complete coaching, embracing the entire athlete for where they are and where they can be, and something that I try to improve every season.

As a Varsity coach, I have often looked at my group of 40-50 players and realized that I was not getting to know them well enough. While I knew my varsity players really well; I was still spotty with the JV players' names because I didn't spend much time with them. One year I decided this was ridiculous, being bad with names is not an excuse; these kids want me to know them and it's important to them. I made a promise to get to know every player's name in my program by the end of the first week.

I bought 50 headbands and took fabric paint and wrote their first names on them and asked them to wear them to practice the first week. I fulfilled my promise, and I couldn't believe how much more connected I felt with my own program just by making that effort to get to know every single player by name. That simple act of getting their names down quickly and showing how important it was to me, made getting to know them even easier as the season went on and built some great connections as those girls moved up through the program. *They immediately knew that getting to know them individually was important to me and the walls came down making our team much more open.*

Study the game, study your opponents, study and create your practice plans, but don't leave out the most important asset of all – study your players. Study their why, their how, their insecurities, their needs, their confidence level, maybe even their past team experience. If you've ever been on a team truly connected on a personal level, you know there is no comparison to that experience and the bond that is created. And if you haven't, you're missing out and so are your players.

Let Go or Be Dragged

One of the best lessons I learned in my 30's was to stop holding on so tight. Let go of the outcome. Let go of the belief that outcomes define me. Outcome based thinking would turn me into something I am not, take me off course, and suck me into the pain of living on a rollercoaster that was run by things under which I had absolutely no control. Mind you, that didn't stop me from trying or believing that I was actually handling it all and controlling it.

So, this was a pretty easy lesson, right? If you know me on a personal level, then you probably are laughing right now. I may be a little bit stubborn, I may think I can accomplish just about anything; just tell me I can't and off I go to prove I can. Had someone told me 10 years ago, when I was 29, that I need to stop focusing on things that are uncontrollable, my response would likely have been, "what's an uncontrollable?"

No, I'm afraid not. The lesson was lost on me for years despite it being right there in front of me, until I sat in a hospital bed in the most uncontrollable situation I had ever been in. It was then that I finally came face to face with the truth. I control my perspective, my beliefs, my choices. I do not control what happens to or around me or my family, or my friends, or my teams. I had blood clots in my body. One of them being in my lungs, and I had no choice in the matter. They were there, at the time allowing me to live, but I couldn't take away the risks that came with them or the fears that came with a total and utter lack of control.

I got through that time because I learned to shift my perspective, my choices, my thoughts, and my influences. As many people do after such an experience, I stopped trying to avoid the unavoidable conclusion of life and instead refocused myself on the everyday controllable actions that I make.

What in the world does this have to do with coaching? Ever hold on too tight to that winning streak? Maybe that first impression you're making on your new team and new set of parents? Perhaps you're facing a total rebuild year with the perception of expectations beyond what your young kids can accomplish without total misery? I have. I've been there. I've held on too tight. I've felt compelled to control things that I didn't have a right to control in order to reach outcomes that I lead myself to believe were necessary. I knew that if I had perfect attendance, 100% effort, completely focused and undistracted players who never got sick or injured, learned fast, thought of nothing but our sport, and eliminated mistakes, our team could do incredible things. So that was, maybe not consciously, my goal. Totally realistic for high school kids...or how about those youth coaches with 10 year old's seeking the same thing?

Coaches want to win. And yes, parents and players enjoy a good win, we jump up and down and celebrate with total joy, especially on a hard earned one. **But survey after survey, and clinic after clinic has shown that our players and families value EXPERIENCE and DEVELOPMENT over winning, trophies or titles.** That stress to win is something that we multiply in our heads as coaches, something that's not nearly as present, despite how it feels. We are holding onto an outcome as though it defines us. Sometimes we're just holding on too tight.

What does letting go look like? Define honestly what controllables are for you, your players and their families and hold those accountable. Define uncontrollables and let those be what they are, move on. That conflicting band concert with your game is not a controllable. Forcing that player to choose between the concert and the game is like asking a kid to choose between parents. It's not a fair scenario and the driving motivation behind that guilt trip on the player is because it may affect an outcome; a win. Or it goes against our 'your team is number one in your life' mentality.

High school and youth kids are going to sometimes miss practice, have off days, not feel well, have conflicts, and play a fantastic one game and tank the next. Some parents are going to be difficult and drive you crazy. Some of the players are going to have trouble learning, focusing, and others will be natural athletes. Some years you will have more of one and less of the other; some years that will be a blessing and some years it will be a curse. Unless you're scouting from the nation's top talent pool, you can't control it. You can't buy yourself an indoor facility and compete with those who can and you can't funnel money into your program that isn't there. You can't make your job that pays the bills leave you alone so you can deal with coaching extras. You can tear your hair out all season trying if you really want too but I don't recommend it. Practice this: "This actually, in the big picture, isn't really a big deal." Feel better?

I remember watching a coach I really respect lose a very big game. He never loses, so I thought *wow I'm really curious how he will handle this loss. I bet he losses it, I bet he just losses his mind because he's so competitive and this never happens and they totally should have won. The ref calls were horrible, the other team was playing dirty, there were so many things going against them.*

Nothing. He was disappointed, talked about how the other team played well, and then focused on preparing the next season to avoid the same pitfall and he moved on.

Sometimes you win big and sometimes you fall short.

It's part of competing. I wasn't expecting that, it didn't fit my perception of a truly competitive coach. And it made an impression on my perspective about how this all works. *Wait, its ok to lose, to publicly fail???*

10 years ago, I would have been spending sleepless nights agonizing over the loss, the mistakes, the lack of control. That extra day off we shouldn't have taken, the spring break practices we should have had, that field trip that left us without a player. But I was emotionally drained every season trying to keep all those loose ends tied, only to fray anyway time and time again. Trying to stay positive was always a struggle for me when I had this conflicting motivation to control that winning outcome no matter what.

Let go. It's incredibly freeing, and once I let go, I never regretted it for a second. Every once in a while, I feel myself starting to hold on too tight, but it's not long before I put it aside and focus on the process, the efforts, the *use what I've got and do the best I can with it* attitude that has been a freedom I know many other coaches need to feel. I can see it and I can feel it when I see another coach holding on too tight and I'm almost willing them to just let go. They're good coaches, but they're conflicted with control vs. process. The kids want you to know them, see them, believe in them, develop them, and push them, but not break them

Let go or be dragged. You're not controlling it when you hold on too tight; it's controlling you.

Sport in the Purest Form

I've met a lot of teams over the past few years with inspiring stories. Some of these stories are inspiring but also heartbreaking, like Team 8 playing for Jamie McHenry's memory. But tonight, I got to be inspired in a whole new way.

I went to grab a bite to eat with my husband after a meeting, and as we sat there I was completely distracted by the chatter and uncontained joyful giggles coming from the back corner of the restaurant. My husband, Sean, kept looking at me with that look he gets when he knows I'm in another world.

"I'm sorry, I have to go talk to them", I said as he gave me that knowing nod he always gives me when I'm on a mission and pulling out my notebook.

Sometimes, to truly appreciate something, you must see it in its purest form. That is what caught my attention, that's what grabbed my heart. Something that's been missing on the ball fields, basketball courts, and turf lately.

I love youth sports; the competition, drive, opportunity and excitement. But it's been spoiled, watered down, tainted, by the greed, power, jealousy, recruiting, bragging, entitlement and business of it all. When you go to a game you learn take the good with the bad and filter out some of those unpleasantries if you can, though you may need earplugs to do it. Then you put on that happy face and try to focus on the good stuff, the parts of sports that are still fun and good.

The last time I felt this strongly pulled to a sports culture in front of me was seeing team 8 gather around Jamie's jersey and take the field in his honor. But tonight, it was there again, and I wasn't even on a field.

Youth girl baseball players, all sitting together with the most contagious smiles and laughter you'll ever see, celebrating their last game over some ice cream. It didn't matter what I did, I couldn't help but catch the smile myself and eventually I had to go meet them. This team was a part of the Miracle League. A local chapter of a national organization that gives kids ages 3 and up, the opportunity to play baseball regardless of ability. Verbal, non-verbal, autistic, physical difficulties or not, they were welcome to be a part of a team.

Confessions of an Imperfect Coach

I spoke with the team coaches, who were also parents of players on the team and they told me their story. One of their daughters would be able to participate in whatever she wanted, but they feared their other daughter would miss out and be unable to play sports. Because of this incredible league, no one misses out on what sports can do to enrich a kid's life. Both of their daughters get to play!

After speaking with these incredible athletes, I took away a lesson I'd have never learn from those super star travel teams I see all the time. These athletes in the Miracle League are a part of something so much bigger, with the purest form of love I've ever seen. They love the game. They love their teammates. They love being out there. They aren't distracted by the things that have crept into our youth sports because all they know is LOVE.

These athletes could come to our fields and teach us to remember exactly what joy and becoming a part of a team is all about, and they could do that just by letting us watch them play. Perhaps we've forgotten the power of WE GET TO. What we take for granted, spoil, take advantage of- those are the things that so many others are just thrilled to GET to be a part of. We need to find that in all of our sports once again.

These awesome kids let me come over and crash their end of season celebration. Here's their picture, playing together for the past 6 years, and best of friends. Go ahead, try to not smile and fall in love ☺

Confessions of an Imperfect Coach

Effective Practices &
Successful Seasons

There's more to teams than Starters and Bench Warmers

Defining Roles for a Positive Experience for All Players on your Roster

Kids who don't understand their purpose, why they aren't playing, how specifically they can improve or change their role on the team, become discouraged and often just stop trying somewhere around mid-season. Without that connection and communication to our players, it's hard to re-engage a player who feels unimportant on their team.

Teams are made up of people who have different roles reaching for a common purpose, but our sports teams often lack the structure and communication to help our players learn about each role. Often our kids don't understand the roles available, where they fit in, or how to work towards a different role if possible. They see the options only as **starters and bench warmers**, when in reality there's a long list of roles – each vitally important to a team's success.

- A high school team will have different and more diverse roles than a youth team, and those high school teams often have the most discontent among players and parents because of it. Roles will include finishers – those players who can take the hard work of the players on the field and end the play with a score
- ball Shuttlers – those who get the ball from the Defenders who skillfully have turned possession over and brought it to the Finishers, or the
- Playmakers
- Defenders
- Communicators
- Face Off/Draw Specialist
- Feeders etc.

There are other roles as well, that are rarely defined or understood on a high school team and that often lead to discouragement, parental and player frustration, and problems as the season progresses. These roles include the Relief Player – the one that comes on the field when the Finisher or Communicator or playmaker need to rest and recharge, who must maintain possession of the ball and keep the quality of play up while those players are out. There are developmental players who have the role of learning as much and as quickly as possible at practice so that one day they will be ready to take over the roles of Playmakers and Shuttlers and Finishers.

There are other roles unrelated to playing, like Leaders, Encouragers, Motivators, and Organizers. Often players have more than one. They may be a Playmaker on offense but training to become a Defensive Communicator where the team will need them next season. They may be a Relief Player who is also a Motivator and Organizer. The question is, do our players know what their role is? Do they understand what they are responsible for, why their strengths have brought them that position, and why it's important? Do they know the path to having another role if that's an option? Can a Relief Player become a Finisher, and is there feedback outlining what they would need to do to reach that goal? Can a Relief Player lose their role and do they know what's required of them to keep their position? What if they are making strides towards a different role or maybe they're not fulfilling their duties, is there a conversation happening to keep them or redirect them to moving in the right direction before frustration moves in?

Keeping the team moving together, striving to be the best they can at their own roles, lowering frustration and challenging each player no matter what role they play are all parts of a successful program. *There's a high turnover on coaches, as well as players hopping programs as they seek to avoid frustration these days.* Lowering that frustration and increasing connection and communication at every level is going to prevent many of the main issues that can tear even the best coached or most talented teams apart. Here's how you can connect with your players this coming season!

1. Define the roles on the team, what are they, why they are critical, and what's expected of each role.
2. Can roles be switched once the season starts? Make a clear path to this process if it's an option. Perhaps an aspiring Finisher needs to perform a certain way at practice (demonstrate clear understanding of cutting to get open for goal, protecting the ball, taking more shots and scoring during drills) A Shuttler may need to meet

Confessions of an Imperfect Coach

certain conditioning goals, ball handling and appropriate hand off decision making.

3. Appoint certain times for players and coaches to connect through feedback, either mid-season, every two weeks, via a quick written evaluation as needed, etc. Or offer open office times certain days of the week where players can come talk to coaches for feedback and get advice on how to work on weaknesses as well as where they are excelling and improving.

4. Make it known on a regular basis that every role is critical to team success, try not to focus praise on one role over another. A Relief Player that keeps the ball in possession, has a defensive stop, or just completes passes and makes successful cuts or ball movement while they are in a short time should receive the same praise as a Finisher after a goal when they come off and when they're on the field, or even at practice the next day or when the game ball is handed out at the end of the game. Consider making your end of season awards about who really mastered their roles rather than goals, stats, and plays.

5. Make sure developmental players understand from the beginning that their role is to learn, then call attention to new skills they pick up and improvements at practice to build their confidence and lower frustration. If they get a chance to try out those skills in a game, offer praise for efforts and keep them motivated to move into that new role later as they get ready for it. Talk to these players during games, ask them questions and give them a chance to show you they are learning and know what they are looking at as well as keeping them engaged in the game they are watching.

Kids often get lost in confusion as line ups change from week to week, or maybe they just can't seem to get on the field. As a parent, I struggle watching my own kids not understand the rhyme or reason behind who plays when; and as a coach I've watched engaged but struggling to keep up players lose heart and stop trying mid-season. *Clearly defined roles, equal importance, and a clear path to understanding how to work towards the role they want to have can keep kids engaged all season long, and keep kids striving to improve in a growth mindset.* It will also assure parents that kids don't play based on favorites or politics, that there truly is a system in place and it's designed with all the players bests interests as well as the overall success of the team in mind.

Are You Willing to Lose, to Win?

Gut check time. Time to ask the questions that make us feel a little bit uncomfortable.

Are you willing to let a win slip by in the quest for a better team at the end of the season when playoffs roll around? Not just hypothetically, would you really do it? With the parents in the stands watching, the kids on the bench behind you with zero stick skills and some of them staring off into space, the opposing coach yelling onto the field ferociously seeking the big W and putting in their best of the best alone?

I can say that in all my support and love of growing the game, and developing players, I still have let my ego steal my team's potential away. It's so easy to identify a win with success, it's human nature, it's taught to us from the generation before us. Our society celebrates it and lifts it up on a pedestal. Not many awards go out to coaches for having a well-rounded team that loses all season. If I can get the ball to Susie and she can drop it in the net on any goalie in the state, then who's checking my winning ego and telling me that I'm sacrificing the development of 16 or 17 other players in search of something that will make ME look good?

But it's more than that, more than needing that win. I'm hurting my team if I seek the almighty win and use that as a measuring stick for success. Because that team that won all season has a shallow bench as the players who weren't very good never got the playing time they needed to get better, my star could get injured or miss a game or be shut down by the other team, and then what do I have left?

Ever wonder why teams that go undefeated in the regular season and seem like a shoe in for playoff success get knocked off in the first round? I used to wonder that all the time, and it happened to me. It was an awful way to end an almost perfect season of Wins across the board.

I had an interesting conversation recently with successful Milton High School Head Coach, Tim Godby that really clarified what I already knew but hadn't quite fully committed myself too. I rarely find a person who is more entrenched in the world of lacrosse than I am, who spends more time growing the game, thinking about the game, building the game, and then personally attending everything and anything lacrosse related. Going further than that, as a female coach I think it's fair to say that I suffer from what most of us female coaches suffer from – an automatic chip on our shoulder for male coaches in women's lacrosse (but that's another subject entirely for later). But I have found that when Godby – who almost impossibly is on the lacrosse field more than I am, talks about lacrosse, I listen, and I always pick up something that helps me get better as a coach.

As a team that wins repeatedly, I wanted to know, how do you keep your team motivated year after year? My teams seem to do great the first year – working hard, racking up incredible winning streaks, driven to succeed, but then they work less hard the next year, and it declines further the year after that. How do you avoid complacency, that feeling that you have arrived and no longer need to put in the grind that's needed to maintain success?

The answer: Milton plays teams that could mop the floor with them during the regular season, even though that's becoming a harder quest as they must now travel far and wide to find teams that have that kind of skill. They aren't afraid to lose, because when they do – they learn, get better, get stretched, and here's the big one – they stay hungry. That team jumps up and down at each state tournament like it was their first time winning it. I believe that's because they don't waltz through their season collecting winning streaks, they are comfortable risking a loss in order to have the skills they need to maintain their playoff success.

Going further into that ideal, is that being willing to risk a loss when the opposing coach is playing their best players and not subbing, am I willing to put in my third string players even though I know they will drop the ball? Am I willing to sacrifice immediate glory for having a deeper bench at the end of the season with more experienced players? I'm not trying to lose, I'm still seeking to win, but without sacrificing development in the process, and with a bigger goal in mind.

Playing all of our players, playing against teams that could annihilate us – these are risks that could certainly put us on the losing side on the scoreboard. But like investing, the payoff is higher when we put a little risk into it. And what are we really risking besides a bit of pride if we don't get that win from playing only the best of our players, or teams we know are closer to our level? If all of our players get played, and they must work hard against the odds, come to practice hungry to get better, appreciate each goal because it was hard fought, and they all have more experience in competition, would the season maybe be a little more enjoyable for them too?

I was on board with playing good competition because I know it makes us better, but I have often fallen into the trap of following our ranking a little too closely during the season, looking for that 10 goal differentials to keep our power ranking higher, playing mostly the best players because we had a great streak going, using the scoreboard as a measuring stick, looking over that player that isn't good enough yet in favor of someone who maybe needed more rest.

This season I want to reach for more than wins, I want better players – I want an entire team of better players, I want players hungry to work harder, who know they still have miles to go to meet their potential, and who celebrate those hard-earned goals like it was their very first, every time.

ON THE LINE! Finding the Practice Sweet Spot

ON THE LINE! 25 distracted, chatty, vacant expressions looking past you have finally tested your limit. You've tried yelling, redirecting, re-explaining, and calling them out by name; but nothing is working. Performance is suffering because practices are starting to feel like a waste of time. You are dragging them through the season. Where is their work ethic? Where is your sanity? Where is your blood pressure cuff...?

RUN! Run until I'M tired! Run until you think this is important! Run until you care!

Sometimes we are just running ourselves ragged trying to drag our kids to the work ethic we know they need to have in order to be successful, but it's not working, is it? You can't force kids to want something, but we keep trying anyway.

I'm sure by now you've heard about making practices fun, about making them positive, about calling out their successes and not using punishments. But your team needs discipline, not rays of false sunshine thrown their way. What choices do YOU have??? How is being positive going to get them to work harder. I think more running...

It's time to change our drill structure. What we are trying to do is take **Intensity** and throw it at them. Then, if we are nice, we throw in some occasional **FUN** activities here and there to balance our approach. But instead of balance we just send a mixed message about what we are all about. We were raised to see things in an all or nothing process but there truly is a better and more balanced way. Instead of alternating fun and misery, let's build something that addresses the way kids learn most effectively.

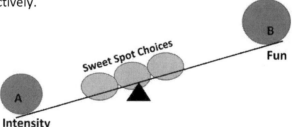

This is the old-school model – One end of the spectrum is a practice that's intense: drills, sprints, no socializing, water breaks in 30 seconds or else, running and push-up punishments, and intimidation. This approach can be effective, but usually not long term. The other end of the spectrum are games that have little point to them other than fun. Also drills that don't have much point and aren't really attended to, it's more like recess and free play and doesn't lend much other than perhaps some team bonding. Lots of fun but now our team stinks... hmm not really what mom and dad are paying for. We can alternate intense and fun but that doesn't really get us anywhere because the kids don't get much out of either scenario. After the fun part, it's impossible to drag them back into any kind of intensity. What we end up with is a seesaw effect – up down, up down- no one ever knows which mode the coach is in until ...GET ON THE LINE!!!!!

OR we can build something all-together new. **I call it the learning sweet spot**, and if you can find it as a coach, your program will **THRIVE**.

Think about your job. When you're inattentive and there's no direction, how much do you accomplish? On the other end, when your boss is breathing down your neck, micromanaging every move, and making you miserable trying to push you to produce more and better work, how does that feel? Not so good, right?

Let's find the sweet spot! As you see there are three options inside that area. You can be perfectly balanced, more fun, or more intense. But you always stay inside those lines so that the learning never stops and the kids never say they've had enough.

First you must ask, what skills do we need to improve on the most right now? Perhaps it's ground balls – a safe bet for almost every team. I can throw them into game-like scenarios and make them run until they get it right... (not sure how running improves ground balls, but we seem to like to try that anyway) OR we go back to the beginning and make picking up a clean, quick ground ball a rewarding experience.

EXAMPLE: Starting with a partner, one is the judge and the other is the scooper. Throw a ton of ground balls out on the field. The scooper finds a ground ball, pretends there is an opponent on their left side and box out, scoops the ball cleanly on the first try at full speed and then rolls it out for another person to pick it up. If they do it right their partner/judge gives them a point. At the end of one minute they switch and the partner with the most points stays in and competes with the rest of the team until you have a small group of ground ball winners. Next step, they are competing in groups of 4 (2v2 competitive ground balls) Build it up until you have 4 to 6 competing against each other.

Why is this different than any other drill you normally do? It's only partially different, but the differences are incredibly important. Think about the elements involved here:

1. A teammate is holding them accountable (something that will benefit them in practice and on the field).
2. They are competing in something that has an immediate reward (getting to continue and compete at the harder level).
3. They are self-motivated to hustle.
4. They are being rewarded only for doing it properly.
5. Attention is put on the skill being done correctly instead of mistakes.
6. It can go all the way to a full game scenario, but starts with the individual mechanics that usually are really at fault anyway, no matter what level they are playing.

When attention can be gained by doing something correctly, players will work harder. Yes, fear is a motivator that can work, but its short term in nature and creates a barrier to performance on the field. A player who has fears about mistakes will risk less, think too much, and freeze under pressure. Or they quit. As a coach, it makes you feel like a shmuck... definitely another con. Why risk that when there's another way?

Players not paying attention? AGAIN? Look at your drill. It may be a great drill, super intense and have all the right skills to practice, but are the lines too long? Is it complicated? Is there any reward or any motivation to stand out? Are they doing the same drill foreverrrrrrr? Is there any fun involved at all?

Practices that balance work and fun at the same time produce incredible results. How do I know this? Because my specialty is rebuilding and starting teams. Because I tried it, repeatedly, it's the only kind of practice I now run, and it never fails. No, we aren't running around playing silly games all practice, because I'm highly competitive and my goal is to develop players as fast as possible, and to win.

Confessions of an Imperfect Coach

But every drill has these elements involved or we don't do it:

1. A reward for doing it right (moving on, call out of praise, high five... always!)
2. An element of fun (1v1 to goal, winner must give the loser a piggy back ride back to the line etc.).
3. A limit on time so they have only a short amount of time to get it right and something they have to focus on (motivation to concentrate – like having to count how many steps the person in front of them took before shooting and call it out before they can go after the loose ball).
4. Short lines (multiple drills or stations whenever necessary).
5. Peer accountability (give each other feedback, count for them, direct them, etc.).

Kids will work intensely at fun, so putting an element of fun inside of learning every skill is so much easier than trying to force them to work harder. They have a built-in motivation system but we must use it!

It doesn't take long to adapt your practices to that sweet spot. You know you have it when at the end of practice the kids say, "It's over already??!!" That's a great sign. At the next game when they get excited about taking those skills onto the field and come off the field saying, "Coach I did it!" Well, that's another great sign. When the players start congratulating each other for mastering skills from practice at games, your team is thriving in the sweet spot. Expect great things to happen! At the end of the day, there should be more reasons for high fives than for punishments. They can leave practice sweaty AND smiling. And that goes for you too!

THE Practice PLAN (YOUTH TEAMS):

Station based training means more action, less down time. It means more learning and trying and less watching. It means more conditioning and moving and less standing. Keep them engaged with a fast tempo practice and time goes fast but not wasted.

Break it down

Here's where the whiteboard comes into play. Each station will be written/drawn up on the whiteboard as A, B, C, D, E. In an hour and a half, your practice will look like this:

Start of Practice: (20 Minutes)

1. Icebreaker Game (the hug game is my favorite, but tag games are great too!)
2. Warm up – Lap and Dynamic and go over board
3. Assign groups (divide any way that works – age, skills or just evenly) Use colored stickers, give each group a different color to stick on their stick, forehead, whatever.

Stations: (50 Minutes)

A. 8 minutes (whistle, 2 minute water break before next whistle to start next station begins)
B. 8 minutes (whistle, 2 minute water break before next whistle to start next station begins)
C. 8 minutes (whistle, 2 minute water break before next whistle to start next station begins)
D. 8 minutes (whistle, 2 minute water break before next whistle to start next station begins)
E. 8 minutes (whistle, 2 minute water break, meet back for wrap up)

You could also eliminate the E session and bring everyone together for a game-like drill to put the knowledge from A through D into practice.

Wrap Up Session: (20 minutes)

1. Share something they learned from each station, something they want to improve on, what their favorite station was.
2. Collect balls and cones and put away
3. End on a fun game

Confessions of an Imperfect Coach

TIP 1: Have only an hour? Cut it down to 3 stations and only one fun game either at the end or beginning of practice.

TIP 2: Keep stations simple. Walk around and help each one, or ask a few parents to help oversee stations. BE CAREFUL - make parent volunteers understand they are there to guide and answer questions only. They should not repeatedly stop the action at the station for instruction. Your players need to learn by doing, and self-reflection of what did and didn't work.

Basic tips to keep things MOOOOVING

1. Use a timer, keep games and drills just long enough to get the point across, but short enough that they hope you do it again next practice! Transition fast. Time it, let 'em have that time to do with as they please, they can talk or drink water or whatever - but when time is up they should be racing back as you countdown.

2. Make transitions a competition (I'm closing my eyes and counting to 20, everyone must be on a cone and holding their stick up before I open my eyes, ready GO!) Don't forget the smile ☺

3. Award ridiculous points! 50 thousand bonus points to the person who scoops all their ground balls with their hand at the top of their stick and boxing out. Oh you just lost 1 thousand points for raking the ball because it hurt my eyes to watch it...(don't forget to use your acting skills. Kids rather enjoy the dramatics)

4. Require silly punishments. That was definitely an illegal check, you owe me 3 summersaults before you can get back in this drill, or Go sing a random player happy birthday and get back in line, you have 30 seconds GO! :P

5. Buzz Words Get It Done. Don't talk about it and then show it. Just show it and walk them through it. Skip the part where they stand there and listen to you just talk. They aren't listening (even if they're looking at you...)

6. Be energetic, direct with instructions, silly, relax and make jokes, mess up when you demo, laugh when you drop the ball, high five with reckless abandon, get extremely excited when someone tries something and it works, and make a point of choosing the ones that are

really trying to learn the ones who get to demo, pick a drill, etc. Make paying attention, being brave to try new things even if they don't succeed, and trying hard the coolest thing they do every day so they can't wait to show you how hard they can work.

7. Bring something different to practices that make it exciting to come. Maybe it's Oreos for an Oreo challenge, maybe it's a radar gun for shot speed, running parachutes for relay races while cradling to goal, swimming noodles to chase down people on the field and making catching harder, silly hats they can't let fall off while doing a drill...you name it, if it's something different, they will be over the moon for practice and they will work harder. (I know fun seems so counterproductive but it's not, it's a learning, effort, and focus catalyst!)

8. Start practice with a fun game. It takes just a few minutes and no one wants to be late if the most fun part is at the beginning. If they know they are only missing the warm up lap they won't care if they're late.

9. End practice with a recap, encouragement, celebrations. NOT. RUNNING.

10. NOT RUNNING! (If you did your practice right, they don't need the running at the end, it should have moved so fast from drill to drill with lots of action and no lines that they should be too tired to run anymore).

The Common Thread

.

SO WHAT?!

What's the theme throughout every article I've put down onto my screen over the past three years? I've asked myself that question because it's the core of my mission and my purpose. Without it, I would have to bend my decisions and beliefs around feelings and circumstances. I'd have to live off of the short-term highs of the win, or despair in the short term angst and humiliation of the defeat. That one bad practice would define my day or the direction of the team, that one good practice would be fleeting and unsatisfying.

The theme is love. It's compassion, long term development, and caring. When I feel ego, winning, titles, anxiety, pressure, impatience start to creep in, I can feel a powerful negative shift in my words and my actions. Even with my focus on positive leadership, I get caught up in the winning and pressure culture just like everyone else. I have parents who push buttons that I may react too instead of focusing on a mutual solution. It's a daily choice, focus, and commitment to put the mission first. It's not always an easy one, but the transformation is about a firm, unquestionable belief in the end game. The vision and mission must be so clear that those distractions become background noise, a fly buzzing around, an annoyance, without the power to turn us from our path.

Awareness is key, we all slip, but if we slip and we don't see the posture of our players fall or we don't catch the subtle shifts in the confidence and belief of our teams, then we lose the very positive and developmental culture we are charged as leaders to build.

A coach can design how it looks, how to get it done and how to reinforce the system they put in place. By networking with other like-minded coaches, getting player feedback and having open communication about what's working and what maybe isn't, the program will cement a foundation that is passed along year after year.

Build it around love. Create an atmosphere of awareness and accountability to that mission, and your team will conquer incredible challenges and build something that lasts and is passed on for seasons to come.

Confessions of an Imperfect Coach

Building a Fireproof Culture

Negativity is like a spark, and when your culture is dried up and under nourished it can burn down right before your eyes. Culture takes daily attention to thrive. You can't eliminate negativity, but you can build an environment where negativity just can't grab a hold.

Learn about creating an environment where your team and grow and thrive in my book, FireProof Culture, The 7 Tools of Unstoppable Teams. Go step by step through the process to protect your team from the destruction so commonly blocking groups from reaching their vision.

Now you know my story. You know why, and how I changed my approach to coaching. You know that it works. Now I'm building my manual to help coaches build a strong foundation with their teams and I can't wait to share it with you!

www.kateleavell.com/fireproof

Confessions of an Imperfect Coach

Acknowledgments

I couldn't have written this book had I never experienced the Positivity Experiment. I may or may not have figured this culture thing out, or I may have joined the huge growing number of coaches getting out of the game out of sheer frustration. Not only did Jon Gordon's writing inspire this experiment, but the day he introduced me to someone as Kate, the writer, I saw myself in a whole new light. His incredible patience, positivity, and encouragement have been a blessing in so many aspects of my life. Thank you, Jon! I'm just one of so many who have had the honor to be better because of your mission in life. I am forever grateful.

I huge thank you to US Lacrosse and my CDP trainer admins, mentors, and peer trainers. For giving me a platform, publishing my writing, allowing me to learn and work with coaches across the country, and believing in my mission, I am incredibly grateful.

For my family who puts up with my crazy blogging habits, literally dropping everything no matter where we were if I had a sudden burst of thought that I simply had to write about, talking to random strangers to get new stories, and my kids having their coaches, teams, pictures as constant subjects in my writing. Thank you for always being understanding and supportive through this journey and for allowing me to have a pretty crazy schedule so that I can continue to do what I love to do, coach.

Some awesome people: Jim Thompson, for being everything I hope to be someday in the movement to drive more positivity in our kids' lives, Joe Ehrmann who is as genuine and kind in person as he is in his inspiring, wise writing and incredible book *InsideOut Coaching,* John and Reed at Changing the Game Project for sharing my articles and for inspiring change across our youth sports through your tireless efforts, James Leath for your awesome leadership ideas that you generously share with the rest of us. Matt Percival – one of the best at what you do and most genuine positive leader at work I've ever met.

My pre-launch reading team and friends and family who read this story and offered feedback to make it better. Keith Brisotti, you're the bestest! Bob Panke, for your zest for life and purpose in coaching that is unparalleled, but sorely lacking in our world today. You are my hero! Shout out to Steph Schenkel– my lax bestie! Every one of my twitter buddies, keep sharing your great ideas and enthusiasm!

Thank you to my players who make me a better person every single day. To my amazing blog readers who write me letters that continue to encourage me to use my voice; you are the parents and coaches we need out there. Your devotion to coaching is inspiring. keep going. You're changing the world, one kid at a time! You lift me up when the days get long and things get hard.

Play On!

About the Author

Kate and her husband Sean of 20 years have 3 kids and have lived in various places around the US including Minneapolis, Atlanta, Chicago, Annapolis, and DC.

Kate travels as a Master National US Lacrosse Trainer, and trains locally as a Personal trainer, Golf Fitness Specialist, Senior Fitness specialist and Corrective Exercise expert and coaches a Varsity lacrosse program. If she's not training or coaching, you can find her spending time with her family, writing, speaking, studying, traveling, or doing something outdoors – preferably on a bike with fantastic scenery!

Besides her own experiences as a coach and working with coaches all over the country, Kate has used the experiences of her kids in athletics to drive her purpose in creating an environment that is fit for everyone who loves to play and where coaches can focus on their purpose and their love of the game.

You can book Kate for speaking and workshops, order her books in bulk for teams and large groups of coaches, and reach out with questions at

Kate@kateleavell.com

42635193R00115

Made in the USA
San Bernardino, CA
10 July 2019